Andy as I Knew Him

By

Charles Emil Ruckstuhl

*To Aileen & Milton
with all best wishes

Charles Emil Ruckstuhl*

© 2004 by Charles Emil Ruckstuhl All rights reserved.

No part of this book may be reproduced, stored in a retrieval system, or transmitted by any means, electronic, mechanical, photocopying, recording, or otherwise, without written permission from the author.

First published by AuthorHouse 05/28/04

ISBN: 1-4140-8603-2 (e-book)
ISBN: 1-4184-2670-9 (Paperback)

Library of Congress Control Number: 2004105024

This book is printed on acid free paper.

Printed in the United States of America
Bloomington, IN

<u>Produced and arranged by</u>
Charles Ruckstuhl Co.

496 Boston Road, P.O.Box 678, Groton MA 01450,
Tel (978) 448-5133. Fax/phone (978) 448-2200
e-mail crxtl@greatpoint.net

Andy as I Knew Him
by
His Stepson
Charles Emil Ruckstuhl

~ C. W. Anderson 1891 - 1970 ~
Famous Author of Children's and Adult
Books About Horses, and Illustrator of
Famous Race Horses.

To "Andy's" niece, Phyllis Anderson Wood,
who gave me much support and encouragement
while I was putting this book together.

TABLE OF CONTENTS

PREFACE ix

CHAPTER ONE 1

CHAPTER TWO 47

CHAPTER THREE ANDY'S CARTOONING DAYS 75

CHAPTER FOUR THE LAST BREAKFASTS. 101

CHAPTER FIVE APPLICABLE MISCELLANY. 191

PREFACE

"Andy as I Knew Him" is the story of C.W.Anderson's life as I knew it when he was my stepfather. It is also a compilation of work by him, starting shortly after he finished his courses at the Chicago Art Institute. Although "Andy" was best known for his work relating to horses, this book addresses itself to that part of his life that was involved with me, his stepson, and work other than what was related to the world of equestrians.

"Andy", as my family called him, ("Herc" by his family because of his height of 6' 4") specialized in thoroughbred horses. He wrote about them. He made gorgeous pastels, lithographs and paintings of them. His books and his portfolios of pastels were published by Macmillan and by Harper Brothers respectively. He also wrote books that addressed themselves to horsemanship and its instructional aspects, all illustrated by the genius of his hand. His children's book series, "Billy and Blaze" were among the most popular books of the day, and, surprisingly, still are. Other popular children's books, published by Macmillan, were written by my mother, Madeleine, and illustrated by Andy.

Chapter one is the heart of this book while chapters two, three and four add those talents and turn of mind that Andy possessed that were not generally known to his public. Chapter four details the poems Andy wrote daily to Madeleine, his wife and my mother, during her last days as she suffered the terminal effects of mitral stenosis. These 41 poems portray not only Andy's sense of humor, but also allow us to witness his undying love for Madeleine, right to the last, 41st day.

Chapter three lets us see not only Andy's dry sense of humor, but also how his portrayal of horses changed over the decade represented here – all during the era of sophisticated New Yorker type humor from a bygone mentality.

Chapter two is similar to chapter three but it contains all original never before published light, humorous poetry - doggerels and art by Andy. The drawings were made with light orange crayons over which the poems were typed. This made for difficult reproduction as you may observe, but that sense of humor remains paramount, much to our delight.

Andy circa 1955 at a book signing session in Philadelphia

CHAPTER ONE

<u>Oh, Those Days!</u>

I wish that everyone could have experienced the high spirits that permeated life in Manhattan back in 1927 when I first knew "Andy", C.W.Anderson. Although I was only nine years old, I witnessed and remember a time when the whole human race seemed to be on a roll toward Utopia. The era of heady possibilities had begun around 1925 and continued one giddy day after another until the stock market crashed in October of 1929.

Meanwhile, redhead Clara Bow, the flapper of flappers, dominated a lively Broadway that echoed the music of the Charleston that had become the rage along with knee high skirts. Speakeasies were everywhere and the popular highball at parties was bathtub gin and ginger ale. You didn't have to be a millionaire to afford a drink - alcohol was tax-free and no one was looking. Carrie Nation was history.

Nestled among the narrow streets of Greenwich Village were two outrageously successful speakeasies, The Pirate's Den and The Blue Horse, both owned by a fellow named Don Dickerman who hired a little known collegiate musician from "down-Maine", complete with megaphone, to play at the Pirate's Den. Rudy Vallee was an instant hit and soon became renown with his "Connecticut Yankees" band. In these early days, before Victor signed him up for good, Vallee recorded on Harmony records as Frank Mater.

Dickerman owned a camp on Lake Kezar up near Fryeberg, Maine. It wasn't the kind you might think: there were no children. The patrons were friends of camp owner Don Dickerman, wintertime habitues of the Pirate's Den and the Blue Horse. Camp Kezar is where our story begins.

In the Beginning . . .

Miss Alvina Walker and my mother, Mrs. Madeleine Paltenghi Ruckstuhl had recently returned from a year in Paris where they studied art and once in a while attended raucous affairs such as the yearly "Bal des Qu'atz Arts". Banned decades ago, this ball, or orgy, was featured in Gene Kelley's 1951 movie "An American in Paris".

Alvina had returned to the U.S. considerably earlier than Madeleine who didn't especially want to come home. Her affection for my father, her ever-providing husband, had long since ceased and my term at Ecole Ile de France wouldn't be finished until December, an excuse for Madeleine to see a little of Europe by herself.

Fate interrupted the stay in France when Madeleine, who had decided to return to art class, fell off a stool, and detached a retina in her left eye. The accident commanded a quick return home just before Christmas, 1925. Now partially blind, Madeleine had no choice but to go home. That was the end of more than a year in France, a period during which I began to speak only French. It had taken me four months to make the switch to French, and on my return to the U.S., another four months to change back to English.

Alvina, who had been in art school in Manhattan with Madeleine before Europe, was happy to have her back stateside. Alvina had met Andy a year or two earlier. It so happened that her new husband, Paul Ickes, a friend of Don Dickerman, had made plans for the summer of 1926 that included a stay at Lake Kezar. The newly weds thought it would be great sport to invite Madeleine to the camp so she could make some needed new friends. Her entourage was limited after 18 months in France and what they thought was her somewhat restricted life: husband, child - that's how they saw it. Logic suggests to me that Alvina knew Andy would be at Camp Kezar - perhaps at her behest? But I am not sure she knew the fire she might be lighting.

So the stage was now set for Madeleine Ruckstuhl to meet a bachelor named "Andy", C.W.Anderson.

<u>It Wasn't So Tough For Some.</u>

"Mr. Anderson" eventually asked me to call him "Andy". It wasn't easy to break the old habit because at 15 I had known him almost eight years, half my life. I too, got a new name from Andy at that time, and it stuck for the rest of my life: Chan. "Chan" didn't stand for "Charlie Chan" but rather, it was a contraction of the name "Chandu the Magician". "Chandu" was a popular program on WOR in Newark, New Jersey and could be received clearly at our distance in Mason because I had learned how to tune a long antenna. Andy thought this was magic - and thus the name that has stayed with me to this day. Prior to this time, I had always been "Sonny".

Before I met Andy, I knew nothing about this man who, took the place of my very busy father. If there ever were two dissimilar men, my father, Emil, and Andy would take the prize. The only thing they had in common was an undying love for Madeleine.

Emil was a self educated, hard working artisan who worked his way up from an apprentice in the U.S. government printing office to the presidency of his own advertising typography company. He was a man at the right place at the right time. His early love of music, Gilbert and Sullivan, for example, and his ability to play the mandolin and the cornet, disappeared completely as his success in business developed. He seemed to have lost whatever little evocative unconditional demonstration of human sensitivity my mother craved but never really received. Emil was German.

Charles Emil Ruckstuhl

Andy was distinctly Nordic, but he had a talent for art and the emotional ardor of a Latin plus a great sense of humor. Madeleine had had her fling at marrying a wealthy urbanite whose desires were fulfilled by a beautiful wife and motherhood. That combination didn't work.

I knew that Andy was born of a Swedish family in Wahoo, Nebraska, and that he taught school early in his life. He also made an unsuccessful attempt to become a violinist. During the summer he worked on the railroad and drove spikes into new ties. He served in the Navy as an accomplished artist-reporter, but during gun practice, he once told me, he almost sank the ship that towed the target! Andy may have been a poor shot and prone to seasickness, but he was brave. Sy Spitzer, a dear friend, and Andy were out on Long Island at Jones Beach around 1927 when a rip tide caught Sy who was no Johnny Weismuller at swimming. Andy saw that Sy was in trouble as the tide distanced him. Andy swam to Sy and with much effort, was able to bring him back to get his feet on the bottom and stagger to safety. Sy never forgot that.

After his stint in the Navy, Andy attended the Chicago Art Institute. He graduated and went to New York to seek his fortune, and, using both his talent and his engaging sense of humor soon was drawing cartoons for The New Yorker, Ballyhoo and The Saturday

Andy as I Knew Him

Evening Post. It's front cover, "Boy Admiring an Apple" from across a barbed wire fence (October 4, 1924) was a big hit. Andy also drew many "Girlie covers" of the day for the American Magazine. His humor for the New Yorker included a cartoon of an Indian sending up smoke signals, asking his buddy "How do you spell 'ugh'?" and a shoe-shine boy asking a passing General "Shine sir?" More seriously, his lithograph, "Changing Times" shows an empty blacksmith shop with seated blacksmith looking at a passing automobile. (I suggested the auto and the title.)

Andy and Sy Spitzer, Cuba, 1929

The New York World Telegram interviewed Andy on May 17, 1932, a time when the depression had affected everybody. Yet, some successful cartoonists were doing very well at a hundred dollars a throw for their product. Andy was providing The New Yorker about one cartoon a week and several for Ballyhoo, a comfortable living at the time. But success of the select group of which Andy was a part didn't come from art alone.

The Telegram quoted Andy:

"Twelve years ago when I was out of art school, Life, Judge and College Humor were the only magazines for comic drawings. Life and Judge were conservative in their standards. The drawings were literal and highly finished and the joke was explained by questions and answers, all printed underneath. We still have three, liberalized.

Moreover, there are The New Yorker, Ballyhoo and Hullabaloo that use between them 150 drawings a month; Bunk, Hooey, Slapstick, Jest, Aw Nertz, Bushwa - you simply can't track of all the newly born or recently deceased publications using the stuff, but it is safe to say the pack uses 500 or more drawings a month and now we have publications like The Saturday Evening Post, Collier's and the rest opening up to it."

The article continued by stating that the primary difference between the new and old comic drawing, according to Anderson, was that the new drawing told its own story. The old was simply an illustration for a joke. European draftsmanship, they stated, had influenced the new [cartoonist] men and women, who in general weren't as literal as the illustrators of the early century.

Andy at Work, 1926

Starkly prophetic, the newspaper's final sentence reads:

"Practically all [cartoonists] cherish the ambition to sling paint in a more illustrious fashion, and some day they are going to have a show of their serious works."

Andy's Family.

The Anderson boys went in opposite directions, Andy to the East Coast and Arnold and Arthur to the west. Andy's real name was Clarence William Anderson but he would never use this name. "Andy" and "CW", or, rarely, "Charles" sufficed. Andy also had a sister but I never heard anything about her until my later life when I came upon a book in 2002 about Booker T. Washington given to "Herk" by "Alice". In it was a mini-birthday card.

Arthur Anderson visited Andy in 1960 at our summer home in Mason, N.H. He brought his wife Beulah, herself a dear person. You could feel the kinship. I thought the two men had quite different personalities. Arthur appeared conservative, pensive, analytical and kindly. Andy was politically liberal, quick to judge (and generally right), outspoken, and he had that keen sense of humor. He also had a keen eye for the girls and enjoyed to the utmost the distilled product of the vintner. He was also one of the best judges of people I ever knew, yet he could be swayed - but only by one person, Madeleine.

Andy at 16

I have a number of letters Andy wrote to Madeleine during these early years, one of which states that he is a pagan. This might have fitted well with Madeleine's personality because many of her notes and miscellaneous letters of the day express her desire to be a gypsy. But, strangely, she returned eventually to Catholicism, her childhood religion from her Italian (actually half-Irish) father. In time, Andy was converted to Catholicism, and that pleased Madeleine much.

And Then It Happened.

Alvina's plan for Madeleine at Lake Kezar must have been for the summer of 1927 because it is the earliest date I have, involving Andy. It is a date on one of Andy's earliest steel point etchings. It portrays my mother playing our square piano in Mason. It must have been drawn in Mason after Camp Kezar where, in a photograph, we see Andy gazing at Madeleine with her face upturned toward him, eyes closed. Although at opposite ends of the gathering, the electric element between the two is clear. Don Dickerman is in the picture along with Jan Streng, a friend of Andy's for a decade or two. Ed Roe, Andy's best friend, is also in the picture.

Ed was a successful patent attorney and I was able to keep in touch with him until his demise around 1970. His wife, Eloise, remarried and recently, just before her death, gave me Andy's pastel portrait of his old equestrian friend, British Captain Marshall. This portrait is being sent to the Museum in Wahoo, Nebraska, Andy's birthplace. We will hear more about Captain Marshall and Andy as we approach the 1950s.

Andy, 1927

Ed and Andy used to meet in Manhattan for some pretty riproaring times. One such get-together ended suddenly in Grand Central Station when, late one night, the two "celebrants" were near a mockup of a Pullman display of an upper-lower berth. Ed perceived it and decided he needed a nap. He started to lie down in the exhibit but Andy tried to deter him and suddenly found himself horizontal on the marble floor with an aching jaw. Ed got into the lower berth. At that point Andy gave up and went home. The next day Ed called him and apologized, saying that the police persuaded him to go home on the last train out to Westchester.

Jan Streng, became a friend of Andy's at art school but Jan's course in life led him to a different but successful career in furniture design. I once visited Jan's penthouse on lower Fifth Avenue and was intrigued with one of his designs. It was the first dynamic type loudspeaker installed in a radio cabinet, aimed downward, 18 inches above the floor. The sound quality was superb for those days. Unfortunately, Jan's wife, Karlin, never enjoyed Jan's patent. She was almost totally deaf.

The Camp Kezar Group. Madeleine, left. Andy, right.

Jan and Karlin, as well as Ed Roe, who was single at the time, visited Madeleine and Andy in Mason quite often. Jan fell in love with the place, bought a house, and became a permanent resident around 1938. Andy, who had just built a granite studio adjacent to Madeleine's property, now had a neighbor from the past. Jan ran into some local complications about ten years later, abandoned Mason and moved to Connecticut, never to be heard from again.

The Real Story Begins.

Madeleine & Andy, Lake Kezar,

Jan and Karlin, as well as Ed Roe, who was single at the time, visited Madeleine and Andy in Mason quite often. Jan fell in love with the place, bought a house, and became a permanent resident around 1938. Andy, who had just built a granite studio adjacent to Madeleine's property, now had a neighbor from the past. Jan ran into some local complications about ten years later, abandoned Mason, and moved to Connecticut, never to be heard from again.

Charles Emil Ruckstuhl

<u>The Real Story Begins.</u>

Madeleine's and Andy's friendship continued after the few weeks at Lake Kezar but late in 1927 my mother developed rheumatic fever that limited her social activity. Andy nevertheless visited her during the day at our apartment on 79th Street. I remember when I first saw him ambling down the long foyer to my mother's bedroom where she lay, stricken.

"Andy Gump!" I exclaimed. Andy let out a little chuckle as he proceeded to my mother's room, but I'll bet he would have liked to give me a good whack. The recollection is not one that pleases me, especially in the light of the good times in the years to come.

Andy continued to do well with The New Yorker and Ballyhoo but I didn't see much of him during the period from the winter of 1927 to the fall of 1931 because of school and camp, school and camp, on and on. I presume mother and Andy saw each other occasionally but my association with him did not begin until after my mother and I returned from Reno in the spring of 1931. I must have seen Andy a few times before that as my diary on Thursday, June 6, 1929 reads:

"Today I won three blue ribbons and two white ribbons (Whites=3rd- -Blue=1st) and a public speaking prize. I had a "fine" time, cleaning out my room. **Mr. Anderson** *helped me."* Summer vacation time had arrived at Riverdale Country School.

Madeleine & Andy, Havana, 1930

Then I saw him again in August 1929 for a few days when he was our guest in Mason. My father and I had come to Mason from New York after camp in July and August. Dad brought the movie camera he had bought for our Cuba trip the previous March with my mother. This was the first year that I spent my spring vacation in Havana. In those movies (now videotaped) I play ball with a very tall, lanky gentleman, Andy.

Early the next year, in 1930, Madeleine, with Alvina, sailed back to Cuba, for more sun, a "remedy" for her rheumatic problem. Dad did not go, but later, on my spring vacation I sailed, this time with my Aunt Carrie (Ruckstuhl), and saw a lot of mother's new friends. Machado was Cuba's president and the Godoys were the bankers supreme. I had to return to school with my aunt but after I left, a picture was taken of Madame Godoy and Madeleine on the beach at Havana - with C.W.Anderson in the picture! I have a second photo of Andy on that same beach, reclining next to Madeleine, admiring her.

A Brand New Chapter.

Andy was helpful in finding a place for us when we returned from Reno in the spring of 1931. I went back to Camp Riverdale that summer (on Long Lake in the Adirondacks) for the sixth and last time before attending the Bordentown Military Institute in New Jersey in the fall. I spent some happy weekends and vacations at mother's 11th Street apartment, a stone's throw from Andy's studio on Washington Square South. I saw a lot of him from then on. We went to a lot of movies when I wore my uniform and relished a hot dog and a soda with him. Mother, Andy and I often went out to dinner, the "Village Barn" being my favorite restaurant-showplace.

One afternoon during my 1931 Christmas vacation, Andy visited us only to become, for the moment, a victim of my early electronic pranks. Prior to his arrival I had rigged up a microphone to our radio with enough wire to let me hide in the closet. Shortly after his arrival, with soft music tuned in, an announcement came over the loudspeaker:

Charles Emil Ruckstuhl

Andy in Mason. 1931.

"Ladies and gentlemen we interrupt this program to bring you a bulletin of terrible importance: Germany has declared war on the United States again. Our ambassadors are being recalled immediately and warfare may begin at any moment".

Andy jumped up, grabbed his hat and coat and exclaimed, running out the door,

"I'm going out and get the latest newspaper about this!"

He returned empty-handed to a pair of laughing individuals. Then we all went out to dinner. In retrospect, I think Andy cooperated nicely with my joke. This time we dined at "Tony, Peter and Martin's", a speakeasy that had turned into a very fine restaurant located at Five East 12th Street.

Andy knew Tony, Peter and Martin because in his earlier days when he first came to Washington Square, he would eat there and pay for his meals by painting murals in the bar area. Those paintings would be a fabulous prize if they still existed. They were about three and a half feet tall and about two feet wide. The Martini, the Manhattan and the Old Fashioned were cleverly depicted ladies in various poses but the one I liked best was the Side Car drink, a "flapper" with one foot on the running board of a roadster, holding the cocktail glass as in a toast.

Tony, Peter and Martin eventually moved to larger quarters right on Fifth Avenue at number 68, and the restaurant was called "68". Tony and Peter passed away but Martin, who was often our guest in Mason (he made a mean "Pink Lady"), lived on and by the late 1950s was bartender at the Penthouse Club on Central Park South. The last time I saw Ed Roe was at the Penthouse Club for lunch. Ed had long been "on the wagon" and Martin made him a "Horse's Neck".

How Not To Start a New Year.

This was the 1932-33 year-end celebration Andy probably thought he would relish above all previous ones. I thought so too because for the first time there would be a group of revelers for me to please with my music idea. The year 1933 would be rung in at Andy's studio at 41 Washington Square South. Madeleine was single and Andy and I were getting along royally. Jan Streng and Karlin would be there. Ed Roe was coming and the humorous, piano playing Hugo Van Arx, editor of "The Nation" would be there. But there was no piano. Instead, I rigged up a set of several radios strategically placed around, all tuned to the same station. It wasn't stereo, but it surely was novel! In those days radio stations used to broadcast orchestras playing at various hotels on New Year's Eve. You would hear no ads, only announcers announcing the next tune. Guy Lombardo got his start along these lines.

And so, the party started around eight o'clock. The studio on the second floor of a small brownstone building was essentially a single room of good proportions. Facing north, its special long, large windows provided the kind of light artists like for work. A small electric grille and a coffee-pot completed the studio kitchen while several couches and a large bed provided ample seating and lounging for guests. A number of lit candles added a mellow glow to the indirect lighting of Andy's amber wall lights. Andy's drawing board, table and easel that usually commanded the center of the studio were conveniently put away in the small utility room for this special occasion. My three radios were placed on the floor in each of three corners and gave forth the soft rhythms of a dance band of a major New York hotel.

By eleven o'clock I had a very uncomfortable appendix. Usually alleviated by ice in the infirmary of Riverdale Country School, the recurring pain, I thought, might be relieved by charcoal if gas was the cause. I knew Bel-Ans were made of charcoal and *adsorbed* gas. We had no Bel Ans but a thought came to me as I asked Andy,

"Mr. Anderson, have you got some charcoal I can eat?" (I would not be calling him "Andy" for another five years).

"Why on do you want to eat charcoal?" he asked, not believing what he heard.

"I think this pain's from gas and charcoal eats up gas. Charcoal's what Bel-Ans are made of," I told him.

"Well sure, but I never heard of eating charcoal. I had a few sticks - hope some are left."

Andy rummaged through a large box and came up with a small one with just six sticks in it.

"Six sticks," he announced, "that ought to be enough. Here, take these. I'll get some more after tomorrow."

I took the six sticks and laboriously chewed each one slowly to a black paste that I downed with a glass of ginger ale Andy had given me. Relief never came.

The party was essentially a success but Andy saw my pain and spared me the effort of shutting off the radios when we all left around one a.m. It was becoming really painful for me to stand up straight. By sheer luck Andy had a friend at the local taxi company and was able to use that friendship by telephone to get us an almost non-existent New Year's eve cab back to 11th street. Normally, we would have walked back. (New York was safe at night in those days). The next night, after a gruesome day, I was taken in a screaming ambulance to a hospital for an emergency appendectomy - in the evening of New Year's Day's.

I had a visitor the next day, Andy. He brought me one of my little radios especially so that I could listen to a very special broadcast on January 5 over WHN, New York.. In those days you spent a week to nine days in bed after an appendectomy. So I heard the broadcast, a 25-minute program of songs sung by Madeleine, accompanied on the piano by Mark Markoff (of later Hollywood renown - Tony Martin's teacher). The program was recorded on three 12" records of which Madeleine gave Andy one and kept two. I have all three but one is worn so badly as not to be acceptable listening. It was Andy's.

Andy played the violin when he was in his teens in Nebraska but he never followed through. He did, however, learn to play the ukelele, actually a little banjo with the strings tuned to "my dog has fleas" (G-C-E-A). He eventually gave me this little banjo and I still have it, complete with the little wooden hand-made bridge he concocted. When I was nine, my uncle gave me a ukelele so that by the time I arrived at this point in my story, I was pretty efficient on the uke. I practiced daily at military school and bought reams of popular song sheet music. Andy and I had a new hobby in common and I actually taught him some chord combinations and transpositions he had not known before.

Andy, Mary, Madeleine, 1938

One day, at the 20 West 11th Street apartment, Andy brought me a blank aluminum precut phonograph disc for me to put on our Victrola and try to record some uke music. I tried it, and it worked! The only problem was that the aluminum wore out the phonograph needle after one recording or one playback, and, to boot, the record was good only for four or five playbacks before it became useless. Good try - but it was a lot of fun.

15

Andy liked jazz and knew most of the popular songs that came out in those days of the 1930s. So did I. But Andy had a few specials he thought were out of this world musically and lyrically. One was Cole Porter's "You've Got That Thing" with a lyric bridge that went like this:

> You've got what Adam craved of Eve
> When he with love was tortured.
> She only had one apple tree
> But you, you've got an orchard!

Andy's second choice for ear-catching verbiage was "I'm Bidin' My Time":

> I'm bidin' my time
> 'Cause that's the kinda guy I'm.

On some summer nights we would sit out under the huge maple trees beside our house in Mason and make up verses to go with one of his favorite ballads,

> "Mamma no like no rice no beans, no coconut oil"
> (Repeat three times)
> "All she wants is handy-brandy all the time"

But we changed it to meet present needs such as the fact that my Aunt Mary Conway (my mother's dearest friend) needed assistance getting up on a horse to ride it.

> Aunt Marie she needs a lift to get on her horse: (Repeat three times)
> And when she's there she has to stay for better or *woarse*."

I could go on for a long while reminiscing along these lines.

The Yellow Peril

Spring vacation found Andy and me walking up Park Avenue to the automobile show rooms that displayed those beautiful cars of the early 20th century. Andy needed a car in which to drive to Mason and declared that he needed an adviser to help him make a choice. Andy knew that I had frequented these showrooms with my friends from Riverdale and that I had foot-high piles of literature on everything from Franklins to the Ruxtons. We first went to the Chevrolet display. That was all we needed. We walked in and there, in the middle of the showroom on a turntable, was the neatest car I had ever seen - a convertible yellow Chevrolet roadster complete with spare tires.

Driving Lessons in the Yellow Peril

"Pretty fancy!" I heard Andy exclaim. Andy always used that term for anything inanimate that was attractive. I heard him say it often enough so that I acquired it for anything I thought was good or great. I used it at military school enough so that it became a fairly common articulation among my classmates! Anything that was "pretty fancy" had to be good, at least in a modest way. Andy had a way with words that could be very amusing, but when he criticized some of the verbiage of the day, his intonation could be equally amusing. I remember him decrying the names of diet crackers, baby cookies and baby cereal of the day.

"Thinsies! Tookies and Bekfus Puddy! My God what'll they think up next to sell something!" he once exclaimed.

I answered, saying that the real world sounded pretty funny too. I cited the original name of the cookie maker, Felber: "The Felber-Gurk-Belch Baking Co."

"That's one they can't help or don't want to!" he answered.

Andy liked the saucy little roadster because yellow was Madeleine's favorite color. He bought it on the spot and named it "The Yellow Peril" - a 1932 sportscar with "free-wheeling", a feature discontinued after a year because of it's very dangerous handling effects.

The summer of 1932 found the "Yellow Peril" in Mason, a five-hour drive at 30-35 miles an hour over Routes One, 202 and the Daniel Webster highway. These routes wound through Connecticut tobacco fields and the centers of New Haven, Stafford Springs and Fitchburg. Superhighways hadn't been invented. Andy conveniently kept his car in a garage in Westport, Connecticut where his friend Perry Barlow lived. Perry was a good friend, an artist and cartoonist for the New Yorker.

Now it was again camp time but this summer, 1932, I would be on Lake Winnepesaukee at Camp Kabeyun, run by a fine man, Mr. Porter. The Yellow Peril came in handy for sporty transportation to Alton Bay with my luggage, tennis racquet and guitar. Andy and I made a two-day trip of it, stopping off at a rest cabin on the way up. Motels hadn't been invented yet. The next day Andy delivered me at camp and then drove all the way back to Mason, a hearty drive, I thought.

Mother and Andy fetched me back to Mason when the camp session was over. Andy had put some miles on the Yellow Peril, driving back and forth from Westport to Mason, but I thought this was an exceptional task for him and Madeleine.

A curious thing happened as we were driving out of Camp Kabeyun. Andy was driving over a grassy stretch by the ball field. Mother was in front with Andy and I was in the rumble seat. Casually glancing at a clover patch some eight feet away, I couldn't believe I was seeing a four-leaf clover. In amazement, I shouted to Andy to stop the car. I jumped out, keeping my eye trained on the little gem, and plucked it from its nest of ordinary clover. It was indeed a big four-leafed clover!

Playtimes in Mason.

The Yellow Peril was kept busy in the summer, both in the early days when Andy visited, and in later days when he resided in his newly built studio, down the road from our house. Andy's granite one-room workplace was built in the late '30s when he moved out of Greenwich Village, Manhattan, to Mason. He lived alone in the studio during its first winter but vowed he would not do that again, living with only electricity plus oil for his hot-air furnace. But he accomplished much on his Billy and Blaze series of children's books.

Andy on Bob, by the Studio

Summers were different. Madeleine was in Mason continuously instead of either Boston or, as in earlier years, her single room apartment in Manhattan (160 West 73rd Street). It was at this apartment that she accomplished so much in the field of music with her singing appearances at Carnegie Hall and Æolian Hall.

Summer meant swimming, and I was around all summer after my last camp year at Kabeyun in 1932. The Yellow Peril received the myriad flexes it would receive over the years 1932 - 1969 on the quarry road that was barely fit for a Jeep. The doors would independently swing open as we purposely drove the wheels over rocks that otherwise would have hurt the transmission. It was "slam-slam" as we proceeded, shutting doors every few seconds - very funny, we thought. I should add that I learned to drive in the Yellow

Charles Emil Ruckstuhl

Peril, Andy at my side. I was 14 in 1932, and would be ready to get my driver's license the next summer – age 15 was enough in N.H.

Andy loved the quarry's cool waters and its pristine setting in the middle of nowhere, a mile or two from town, yet deep in the woods. It was quite a spectacle to come upon if you were strolling through the woods, unaware of its presence. I must confess that Andy's lithographs of the slanting walls of granite and reflecting still waters are masterpieces of melancholy reminiscence for me. What fun we had, shooting floating bottles with a .22! If, in the fall, the weather was a bit nippy, Andy always had a bottle of sherry for all to share and keep warm, with or without a reason - for medicinal purposes.

In 1929 when we more or less discovered the quarry, huge one-and-a-half inch galvanized steel cables still supported members of the original tall standing crane. It was used in Mason's halcyon days before the quarry went bankrupt over a granite obelisk they could not deliver as priced. Tom Rhodes, Mason's beloved old timer who worked in the quarry back in 1890, used to tell about the crew quitting and blowing up the safe in the post office shack. They also left the giant wood-fired boiler go over-pressure and blow up, taking the granite building's roof with it. The distorted safe and boiler were still there until just before WWII when scrap steel prices rose, and things like boilers in the woods disappeared.

Sharpshooter Andy, 1937

The beautifully constructed 100 foot tall brick chimney still stood firmly as did the walls of the boiler house that

20

provided steam for the machinery, now some 30 feet under water. But Andy thought, and quite correctly so, that the derrick should come down now, and not at some random time. The base block, a huge chunk of iron-braced chestnut, measured about three by three feet and about five feet long. It was beginning to sag over, making parallelograms of its ends instead of squares.

Early one bright morning Andy, alone in the Yellow Peril, went over to the quarry with a long broomstick and a hacksaw securely tied to its end. He climbed up to the highest point in the quarry, overlooking the water, opposite the granite landing on which stood the derrick's weakened foundation. There, he started hacking the longest cable of three that supported the forty-foot main derrick member. This might have been a perilous procedure except that the old cables weren't taut. As a result all went smoothly with no snapping or flailing as the giant wooden mast went crashing.

How I wish I had been there! But Andy knew he was trespassing to accomplish this absolutely necessary feat. In all probability no one would ever know who did it, or when it was done. Thus the quarry was made safe for us - the only people who dared swim its cool, soft waters,.

The direction in which the mainstay landed was straight back in the woods, just as Andy had planed it. Only a few unmovable cables lay around, well out of the way of swimmers or divers. No one ever complained about the "unavoidable" event. I don't think there really was anyone to complain because before we swam in those waters, no one in town dared go near because of the persistent rumor that there were water moccasins around! I think Andy dispelled that falsity quickly.

By way of a quick background: the quarry remained essentially waterless until 1914 when the dammed uphill pond, used for water for the big boiler, was released after a torrential rainstorm. The abandoned dam gave way and at least eight million gallons of water came roaring through the woods down from the high pond (about 1/8 mile uphill), into the empty quarry - just about enough water to fill it to the brim. The quarry stayed full from then on, the springs that nurtured the original two or three feet of original water being able to balance evaporation from the newly formed granite-lined pond.

The chimney stood about 90 years until it was taken down around the 1980s by some new owners of the property, Lunar Associates. Gone were the days when I used to get into the chimney and shout upward to hear its deep resonance. Gone are the old days when few knew of the quarry that now, according to stories, sports a yellow Volkswagen on its bottom. Gone too are the three buildings that housed the workers. I remember those houses. One of them had a horse's skeleton on the second floor. The poor creature apparently climbed up the abandoned house's stairs and couldn't get back down. Andy painted those collapsing houses - another masterpiece on canvas. This area actually had a name: MacDonald and the MacDonald Quarry. Rand-McNally showed it on New Hampshire maps until 1932

Horses and More Horses.

Peter, Bobcat, Wise Bug, Joker, Suzie and Howdy: those are the names of our horses in Mason over the years. In 1929 "Peter" was my mother's first horse, the horse Andy met first. A Mr. McConville brought him from Boston to Mason for Madeleine to ride. He would be kept in our new barn, built on the foundation of our old barn that had gone beyond repair. I fortunately learned to ride on Peter because I would spend many hours on a horse - two years later in the deserts around Reno. That horse was "Honey" a mustang I learned to love dearly.

One or two summers passed before Mason's endless dirt roads would see Andy riding Bob (short for *Bobcat*), a fine horse owned by Dr. Boynton in neighboring West Townsend, Massachusetts. Aging Dr. Boynton no longer rode ten-year old Bob, so Andy's use of the beautiful chestnut was a pleasure for both owner and rider!

At about that time, we stabled a young mare named Susie. She was more or less my steed because I fed her and groomed her fairly often and I was proud of her. One warm afternoon, while a cocktail party was being enjoyed on our front lawn with our guests, I decided that this was the perfect time to show off Suzie in her best form. I had not ridden the mare in several days, so she was feeling her oats and ready to go when I simply put a halter on her, led her outside, and jumped on her back, headed up the field toward our house. Little did I anticipate the dangers ahead as we slowly ambled over the field and up to the road. With no saddle to insulate me from every muscle in her back, I pulled the halter to the right and she turned down the dirt road, toward the house and the revelers.

Andy on Bob (Bobcat). 1940

I am not sure I ever sat on a Diesel engine when the accelerator was "floored", but I certainly felt some thing like that when Suzie suddenly decided to gallop, full tilt, toward the house. I swear we were going 50 miles an hour as we approached the house and all the guests. I saw Andy and shouted to him,

"I can't stop her! I can't stop!"

If he answered me, I didn't hear it for all the cheering.

"Bravo! Bravo!" they all shouted, thinking this was great show while all the time I was panicking as to what to do before we reached the steep hill where the road went down by Andy's studio. I decided not to go down the hill, but rather take the short but blind driveway leading up to the neighbor's house. I could see Susie stopping short as the house and garage appeared, and me doing a somersault over her head into the sky and who knows where else.

I pulled the halter hard to the left and Susie started up the driveway.

"What the heck," I thought, I might as well chance abandoning Susie for soft ground. So I jumped off. My only problem was that as I flew through the air, the "soft ground" gave way to a wall of fieldstones that I hit mercilessly on my left side. I began to cough up blood and my left arm was no longer in my control.

Andy rushed up, saw me and helped me get up. The pain in my left shoulder was excruciating. I recall little after that except that I had a very quick ride to the Burbank Hospital in Fitchburg where they found that my only real problem was a broken left arm. It was broken only a half inch below the shoulder socket! This was a strange place for a break, but they rigged up a crutch-like brace with a big paddle that looked like a schoolroom chair with writing arm.

I was home again that night, not the hero I had wanted to be, but rather a self indicting idiot who in the first place should have simply pulled hard on the halter and stopped my beast before she got completely under way! So, a month later, after pain followed by ceaseless itching, the contraption and cast were removed, much to my joy despite the offense to my olfactory organs at the moment of the new arm's revelation. Whenever I buy a new suit or jacket, I am reminded of this event and Andy's rescue because the left sleeve must always be made a quarter of an inch shorter than the right. It seems my left arm stopped growing that summer! End of case!

One day, during the next summer of 1934, Andy and I planned to meet on horseback at what used to be the Townsend "poor farm", half way between Mason, New Hampshire and adjacent Townsend, Massachusetts. I headed south from Mason on Howdy, the horse I rented from a nearby farmer friend. The horse was conveniently stabled about a mile down the road toward Townsend. Andy headed north from Townsend, where a neighbor had driven him to pick up Bob. Andy had not driven the Yellow Peril to Townsend because Bob was coming up to Mason to stay the rest of the summer at our barn and pastures.

Andy as I Knew Him

We met near the "Poor Farm" to trot around some wide, cleared pastures, and bring Bob to Mason. Bob had stayed in Mason before and knew his stable in our barn. We started to romp across the fields toward a forest when a terrible thing happened.

Bob suddenly reared. Andy fell off backwards, slightly off to the side of Bob, catching his balance so as to land standing, but stumbling. I could see heavy wire tangled around Bob's left rear hock. It was old telephone wire. Bob went down on his side, thrashing as the wire became taught around his groin. It cut deeply into the muscle. Blood spurted from a deep gash. Andy, unhurt, shouted to me,

"Get back. Stay away. Don't come near!"

Bob appeared to become disentangled as Andy tried to grab his bridle or martingale, all to no avail. The poor horse did manage to get up, and then, to our amazement, he darted toward the Townsend-Mason road and headed for Mason! I had backed Howdy safely away when Andy, at the top of his lungs, called to me,

"Follow him back and see that he gets into his stall. Have your mother call the vet. Then have someone come pick me up. If there's no one, you know how to drive. HURRY!" I got the message and headed off at a full canter.

In retrospect I think Andy should have mounted Howdy himself, and let me walk back. It was only a few miles, yet Andy's six-foot-four body would have been a bit heavy for my horse. Also, I was glad to have the chance to drive Andy's car.

I took off after Bob. By now he was out of sight. I rode Howdy hard, at a fast canter until he was puffing, but I didn't let down his pace as we followed a trail of blood all the way. Howdy and I covered the distance back in record time without catching up to Bob. I was worried about Bob's whereabouts when I reached the barn where the Peril was parked, but Bob was already waiting by his stall! He had headed to his favorite place, wounded, with much loss of blood, yet the tendon was not severed. Rather, the wire had cut into the skin and had run parallel to the tendon, cutting a flap in his flank.

My mother saw me return without knowing Bob had preceded me. As she opened the front door I called out to her and let her know what had happened. She took care of the rest. I tethered Howdy to the birch tree next to the barn and zipped away in the Chevy, headed for Andy. He was already a mile or so toward Mason when I spotted him, stopped, and told him what I had done. When the two of us got back to Mason, a veterinarian had been called, and was on his way from Fitchburg. An hour later, Bob's leg was clean, sutured, probably numb, and bandaged. A month later the wound was well on its way to recovery. Thus ended an event that could have been much more serious.

Sixty years later, at a dinner party in Ayer, I met a man to whom I told this story. He was from Townsend and had known Bob's owner, Dr. Boynton. He well remembered a horse by the name of Bob - a chestnut, still in good health just before World War II! Dr. Boynton had passed away by that time and Bob belonged to someone else, I was told.

"Did this 'Bob' have a big scar on his left rear groin?" I asked.

"Yes, he did, but no one knew how he got it," was the reply.

He knew now. It *was* Bob!

A Different Kind of Steed.

I didn't know it at the time, but 1934 would be the second summer of bone-breaks for me with Andy, as usual, to the rescue.

A young fellow whom I knew at the brand-new Spaulding High School in Townsend had fixed up a model T Ford as a sort of buckboard, and was running it around his parents' fields with great glee. But he had another, and this one was for sale for $15, and I just happened to have a sawbuck and a fiver for the Flivver. The kid told me, on the day Andy drove me to Townsend to try out the machine, that the spark control was reversed and the head of the fish on the can of sardines he used as an escutcheon plate was actually advance and not retard as would be normal.

So I got into the buckboard, thrilled to have something to drive. I knew the foot pedals and I thought I remembered the spark settings. So off I went into the rolling fields. I turned at the far end and somehow managed to stall the engine. Without instructions as to how to crank an engine, I got out and, with the spark *advanced*, proceeded to push *down* on the crank. POP! The crank flew up. My arm flew up, and my wrist was up among the clouds, I thought. When I brought it down, I had (on the right side this time), an elbow, and a "J" joint, and my wrist. The "J" joint was new and fitted between the middle finger and the index finger of my left hand. It then turned upward between my index finger and my thumb, and then resumed its direction, straight ahead. It looked funny, I thought, and it didn't hurt. It was numb - for the nonce!

I ran a half-mile back to the house where Andy was waiting in the Yellow Peril. He looked at my arm and suddenly the Yellow Peril became the ambulance it had been the previous summer. The buckboard boy's parents called the Hospital, and Andy and I were off. I was given an injection at the hospital, and put on a gurney. I was sleepy when a doctor took my right wrist between his two strong hands. I recall that I was in a rocket, accelerating toward the moon when I awoke feeling just great. I never felt better.

We returned to Mason in the Yellow Peril, this time with a simpler cast than the year before. As we drove home to Mason at around four o'clock, I asked Andy if we could go to a movie that night in Fitchburg. He wasn't sure. It was just as well. By suppertime the effects of the shots were wearing off and my troubles that would plague me for the next week began. I will never forget, a week or so later, when Andy drove me to Fitchburg for some tests I had to take to enter Exeter. We went up to the registration desk of the High School where the exams were being held.

"Are you left-handed?" the lady-in-charge asked me.

"No, not at all," I responded.

"Well, then can you write as well with your left hand?"

"Not at all," I answered.

"Well then?" came the reply.

I turned around, looked at Andy, almost crying.

"I think we'd better go back home and think this over," he suggested. "Good-bye Miss. We'll see you later."

We were off again, back to Mason. What happened next is another story involving some amazing coincidences not involving Andy. I did get into Exeter, however, after a year. But that's a separate story in *my* biography.

Cupid Enters Our Life.

Andy never quite recovered from the hilarious, yet melancholy, amusement he experienced in Mason one summer afternoon in 1933 when he found a boy, recently turned 15, lying face down on a manure pile. He had been looking for him for quite some time after he had driven our visitor, Helen, a 16 year old girl, over to her mother who was visiting in town. Both were returning that day to their home in Milford, N.H., some 15 miles away. The girl, who fell in love with a military uniform at her June graduation ceremony kissed this young boy and started a romance that lasted a few weeks and sent him into a blind orbit. Shortly afterwards, however, she took a shine to the young boy's visiting older cousin, a redheaded 18 year old smart-Alec. The world had suddenly come to an end for this puppy love affair of a 15-year-old kid.

I must confess that the only time Andy ever gave me a verbal lashing was in mid-June when I nagged and nagged my mother to have Helen visit us again in Mason. That was well before my cousin's appearance.

Andy in Mason, 1941

"You're a rotter. You're a real rotter! Leave your mother alone about this Helen and behave yourself!" he roared at me one night before bed-time. Yet, within that week Andy had driven me up to Milford in the Yellow Peril for a visit with Helen (which turned out to be the last).

The fall of 1933 saw the beginning of a period where Andy's and my paths didn't cross very often. I went to the Townsend (Mass.) high school and stayed the winter of 1933-4 with the Marshall family in Mason, people my mother had known since childhood. Andy and Madeleine were in Manhattan at their respective residences. It was around this time that they thought up the idea of a series of children's books that would be named "Billy and Blaze", stories about a boy and his horse. Macmillan liked the idea and it wasn't long before Andy's second career as an author of children's books began.

Shortly after, Andy and Madeleine decided that she should publish some of her children's stories and have Andy illustrate them. This idea worked out very well and Macmillan published all of my mother's manuscripts. Among her books there was: "Honey the City Bear", "Honey On a Raft", and a lovely story about the goat, "Remus Goes to Town". I have the galley of "Rumpus Rabbit". It was the last of her children's books.

The year 1934 saw me in school at Exeter, N.H. New York would no longer be my home because I would be either at school or in Mason in the summer time. Andy's success would allow him to live in his stone studio that he had specially built, just down the road from our house. It was in the winter of 1936-7 that Madeleine was stricken with bacterial endocarditis and almost passed away. She was bedridden all winter in the Mason house, but most fortunately had had steam heat installed the previous summer. Madeleine had also hired a couple to stay the winter and serve as cook and handyman - a solution to what could have been a big problem.

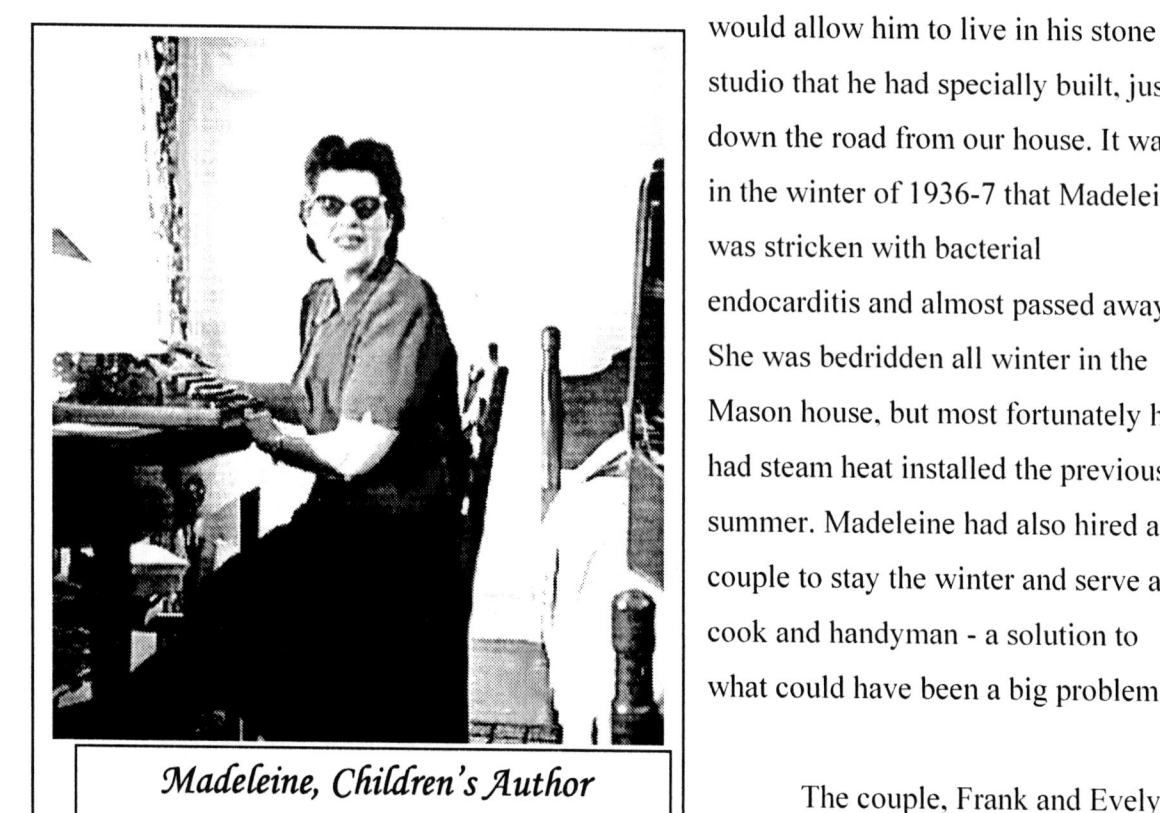

Madeleine, Children's Author

The couple, Frank and Evelyn Boyle were allowed to board their goat in our stable, a goat that Madeleine named "Remus". He became famous the following year because as soon as Madeleine was able to accomplish any writing, (after recovering miraculously, some say), she started the children's book "Remus Goes to Town". With Andy's illustrations, Macmillan published it.

Winters in Mason, although harsh in many respects, were always a warm and friendly refuge for me at vacation time. Mother was home. Andy was home, and I was on my way through Exeter, headed for M.I.T. During one of the few winters we all spent in Mason between 1937 and 1939-40, I recall a very special time or two with Andy. It may have been when mother was sick and confined to her bed, tended by Evelyn, but my memory is not clear. I do remember a huge fire in Andy's studio fireplace. Madeleine was with us some of the time. At other times it was just the two of us cooking a huge porterhouse steak over the fire, with a glass or two of good sherry at hand, and "Tally" our Dalmation, looking on so yearningly. Warmth and friendship surrounded us and the conversation was always lively. Those were golden evenings by a golden fire for either two of us or three, when mother was well enough to be there.

Now the summers began to be joyous. There would be parties. There would be dances, and I had all the electronics to turn a barn magically into a hi-fi ballroom. I had taken my amateur radio examination, passed it and the code test, and received the call letters W1JZD: "Wizard" as Andy read it and confirmed that my name "Chan" (short for Chandu the magician) was indeed appropriate.

The first dance we held was on the 4th of July 1935. I had just returned from Europe with my Aunt - a trip my father arranged for me at Madeleine's behest because of my having been admitted to the Phillips Exeter Academy. Everyone was invited, the Strengs, Ed Roe, and neighbors spending the summer in a house on the same road.

Andy at Work in His Studio with Tally

Andy and I rigged up a crude but bountiful bar from the extra floorboards that lay around. I had two five-foot square Celotex baffleboards hanging from the rafters, each with one of the newly developed 12 inch dynamic speakers at the center - a fairly advanced system for the year 1935, all powered by amplifiers I had built. Everything was just right for dancing, and, to my delight, the neighbors had a niece my age. She was vivacious and knew how to dance. That's how I learned! I remember Adele (that was her name) trying to teach Andy a few steps because he never learned how to dance. His was a slow shuffle not especially in step with the music. Adele gave up, much to my pleasure, after about 15 minutes.

Charles Emil Ruckstuhl

We all went to the neighbor's house around 11 o'clock to shoot off some Roman candles from their clear, high vantage point overlooking the valley. One of the fireballs spewed out by the Roman candles started a grass fire down the hill. I remember that Adele called the local volunteer fireman but that's about all. In a matter of minutes, I was riding with another neighbor, Frank Coyne (a man I admired because he was an M.I.T. graduate). We zipped along at 65 miles an hour toward Greenville to get a fire engine from a fire department that didn't answer!

When we arrived, Frank jumped out of the car, found the fire department garage doors unlocked, opened them, and got into the red monster. He managed to get the engine started, and took off in his hijacked treasure, sirens bleating out a shrill wail. I followed, in his car, back to Mason, trailing far behind.

Andy and Joker. 1944.

When I got to Mason, there was Frank, surrounded by well wishers with flashlights. The volunteers had put out the fire while we were away but Frank was some sort of hero anyway. We all headed back to the barn for a last nightcap, a dance, and a "good night". The Greenville firemen came the next morning to recoup their vehicle. No charges were brought against Frank whom we didn't see until the next afternoon!

Adele would remain a friend until she passed away in 1965 but Andy, in the meantime, taught her how to ride a horse. We all had some great picnics that summer, especially around Mt. Monadnock where we did not bother to climb to the summit. In those days you could go up to the "Half-Way" house, but it burned down later and the road was closed, except to officials.

Back to Horses.

Although Adele, Andy and I never took horseback rides longer that a hundred yards, mother, Andy and I did. We would be gone perhaps an hour, sometimes two. Andy, in the later days after Bob, bought Joker, the beautiful gray headstrong stallion he loved. Mother had Wise Bug, and I had Howdy. When mother did not ride, I rode Wise Bug. It was on one of those rides with just Andy and me that something startling happened.

Andy and Joker. 1944.

It was a warm, rather humid day and the flies were biting if one loitered too much. Andy and I decided to take a ride fairly far afield, over the old deserted Hammond-Elliot road, as we used to call it. Andy was ahead of me on Joker, trotting, as we went through the woods. Wise Bug was in good fettle and seemed to be enjoying the ride too. At one point, a brook crossed the Hammond-Elliot road, but there was an old bridge across it that still supported a man and a horse. It was somewhat moss-covered and blended in with the scenery so as to make it look as if it were part of it. Andy crossed the bridge at a fast trot as I followed. Suddenly, roughly at two-thirds of the way across the 15 foot bridge, Wise Bug went down. Her front right hoof had gone through a plank, but somehow she hit soil underneath and recovered, pulling her hoof up and out, remaining upright. I went over her head, did a 360°

somersault in mid-air - and landed on my feet! Wise Bug was waiting for me to remount as if nothing had happened. I am not an acrobat, so I can assure you this was some sort of miracle. Andy did not see it happen, but when he turned around and saw me standing beside Wise Bug, dismounted, he was incredulous. When I told him what had just happened we both realized that both Wise Bug and I were pretty lucky not to have suffered any broken bones!

Art Class, Baltimore, 1962

Andy had about four English saddles that he used more or less successively, but his fifth was known as a Maclellan. I liked it because it was sort of halfway between a Western and an English saddle. It looked as if it should have a horn, but it didn't. It was split in the middle for about eight inches, providing, I suppose, some ventilation underneath. I don't think Andy ever used it, but the one time I tried it, my horse, Howdy, decided he wanted to dart into a neighbor's barn he had never seen before. In he darted with me on him! The acceleration had me almost flat on his and my back. Luckily so, because on inspection I found the barn's rafters to be dotted with large spikes on which my eye sockets could have been impaled! So much for Maclellan saddles!

Andy's Star Rises Quickly.

Andy's books sold well, both the children's books and the more serious ones devoted to text and portrayals and to portrayals alone. Harper Brothers had come into the picture by publishing Andy's horse portfolios with great success.

Andy began to receive requests to give lectures at libraries, schools and museums that had become acquainted with his genius. The very British Captain Marshall, Andy's friend of many years, visited Mason frequently and showed us his equestrian proficiencies by riding Joker and taking him over jumps in one of our big fields.

Andy and "Marshy", as Andy used to call him, decided one summer day to go together to Maryland where Andy had a speaking engagement in Charlestown, near Baltimore. They went in the Yellow Peril and evidently had a jolly time of it. But something went wrong according to the Baltimore newspapers that gave a story about some major geographical errors on the part of a famous artist. He came to Baltimore to give a talk about horses and drawing and painting them, but it seems that the artist never showed up for his engagement. Instead, he, and Captain Marshall, found themselves in a town named Charlestown on a chilly evening. It was the right town, but it was the wrong state - West Virginia!

The lecture was missed, but, in an attempt to get back to the right Charlestown as soon as possible, Andy attracted a Maryland trooper's attention by his mode of driving. He was stopped and the next thing he and Captain Marshall knew, they were standing in front of a judge who spared Andy the bother of having a driver's license for six months. Maryland and New Hampshire had reciprocal agreements on the subject of DWI, and so, Andy was in a touchy situation for a while. He was allowed to drive back to Mason after a night's rest, but no further. For the next six months, friends, relatives or anyone else who could help, came to the rescue. Madeleine did not drive because of her detached retina from her accident in Paris in 1925, but Andy made out surprisingly well until he could return to normal. He, at least, had no problems for the next six months with DWI!

The years between my college days and the early fifties have merged partly due to the turbulence caused by the second World War, my participation as a Research Associate in antisubmarine warfare at M.I.T., my marriage, and then my child - all in that order. During this time I saw little of Andy, but it was his wish, according to my mother, that she pull things together after a serious rift I will describe in a moment.

Charles Emil Ruckstuhl

My senior year laboratory work was considered very promising by my professor, Dr. R.H.Bolt. As a consequence I was asked if I would take a position as a Research Associate in his newly formed laboratory that was engaged in anti-acoustic mine and anti-submarine warfare. I told Andy about this, and he thought I ought to jump at the offer. I did. Then came Pearl Harbor. Our group under Dr. Bolt received Presidential deferments to do our research both in the laboratories in Cambridge and at sea - in the Atlantic, in the Pacific.

I was not getting along too well with Madeleine as I was off to this and that oceanic rendezvous for testing our developments. As youth would have it, I fell in love with a young girl to whom I was introduced by Madeleine about a year earlier. We decided to get married, but, due to the umbrage taken by Madeleine to my affairs of the heart, I decided not to tell her or Andy that I was headed for the altar. Instead, Peg, the young lady I just mentioned, and I headed off to Plaistow, N.H. and a J.P. for an undisclosed marriage. Madeleine promptly disowned me.

Madeleine & Andy Wedding Day 1944

Eighteen months later, Linda was born, and the tide began to change when Madeleine called me to tell me that Andy missed me and wanted to patch things up. From there on matters improved. Andy's work was now renown and his books were selling well. I had a couple of promotions at the lab and bought a house in Arlington.

One afternoon, in November 1944, the Catholic Priest in Greenville called Madeleine and Andy to his residence "for a chat". During this session the Priest expressed some pretty strong opinions about the advisability of their consideration of marriage. Madeleine had turned decidedly toward the church, and away from her earlier fancies of being a gypsy. She was now a Catholic after some 40 years of absence from the

Church. I presume that Andy, too, gave up his stance as a pagan, but, as he told me shortly after their marriage in December 1944,

I joined to please her.

I well recall the sumptuous dinners at the Somerset Hotel, where Madeleine and Andy had taken up winter residence in the mid-forties. Peg and I were often invited to such occasions when small orchestras and superior performers rendered music, dance and charm during the dinner hours. Success had arrived at Andy's doorstep and would remain there for the rest of his life.

Such was not to be my fate for the moment. I returned to the classrooms of M.I.T. for further studies that required "burning the midnight oil" almost continuously. I received the degree for which I strove, but this was not the stuff of which happy marriages were made, thought Peg. In 1947 she sued for divorce and received our house and other tokens that go with such matters, including support for Linda. Andy understood the situation and backed me all the way, as a good stepfather would.

Andy was perusing the newspaper one day during a period when I was pursuing a career in marketing something that was about to hit the Boston market: television.

"I saw this ad in the paper, Chan," he told me with some enthusiasm. "It's by the Bendix Corporation. Their International Division wants someone like you to set up business all over the world for sonar detection of large schools of fish. This looks like it's right down your alley, and sort of exciting too!" he concluded.

I applied for the job, got it, and found myself spending a month in each coastal country of South America. My Spanish became very useable, aided by my native French.

My first problem, away from home, was hepatitis when I arrived in Venezuela, derived apparently from hypodermics used in New York to give me immunity to various tropical diseases. My phone calls home and my letters, answered by Madeleine and Andy gave me sufficient spirit to be able to hang in there and not take the next plane home. Had I not had this backing, I would never have had the many exciting and adventurous experiences I was so fortunate to have in Venezuela, Colombia, Ecuador, Peru, Chile, Argentina, Uruguay and Brazil. I experienced nine months of travel and adventure, most of the times very lonesome, but, happily, not all.

I returned to Mason in the fall of 1949 to warm fires and good conversation. Andy was progressing greatly with his books, portfolios and private assignments. Here is a list of his published items:

A Filly for Joan	*1960*	Macmillan
A Pony for Linda	1951	Macmillan
A Touch of Greatness	1945	Macmillan
Afraid to Ride	1957	Macmillan
Another Man o' War	1966	Macmillan
Big Red	*1942*	*Macmillan*
Billy and Blaze	*1947*	*Macmillan*
Black, Bay and Chestnut	1939	Macmillan
Blaze & the Mountain Lion	*1954*	Macmillan
Blaze and the Forest Fire	*1948*	Macmillan
Blaze and the Gypsies	*1950*	Macmillan
Blaze and the Indian Cove	*1961*	Macmillan
Blaze and the Lost Quarry	1966	Macmillan
Blaze and Thunderbolt	1955	Macmillan
Blaze Finds the Trail	1950	Macmillan
Blaze Shows the Way	*1964*	Macmillan
Bobcat	*1965*	*Macmillan*
Complete Book of Horses	1968	E.P.Dutton & Co.
Deep Through the Heart	1940	Macmillan
Favorite Horse Stories	1967	E.P.Dutton & Co.

Great Heart	1962	Macmillan
Heads-Up Heels Down	*1959*	*E.P.Dutton & Co.*
High Courage	*1963*	*E.P.Dutton & Co.*
Horse Shoe	1951	Harper & Brothers
Horses Are Folks	1949	Harper & Brothers
Linda and the Indians	*1953*	Macmillan
Lonesome Little Colt	1961	Macmillan
Miracle of Greek Sculpture	1970	E.P.Dutton & Co.
Phantom	1969	Macmillan
Pony for Three	*1955*	*Macmillan*
Salute	*1957*	*E.P.Dutton & Co.*
Sketchbook	*1968*	*Macmillan*
The Blind Conemara	1971	Macmillan
The Crooked Colt	*1954*	Macmillan
The Horse of Hurricane Hill	1956	Macmillan
The Outlaw	*1958*	Macmillan
The Rumbleseat Pony	1971	Macmillan
The Smashers	1952	Harper & Brothers
Thoroughbreds	*1967*	*Harper & Brothers*
Tomorrow's Champions	1946	Macmillan
Twenty Gallant Horses	1965	Macmillan

Unsure data is *italicized*.

Andy not only wrote books for children, books for education and guidance, and book-like collections of his artistry such as "Deep Through the Heart", he also created albums or portfolios of portraits of horses of all descriptions. These portfolios are priceless collections of perfection, each with about a dozen portraits, all but two in full pastel color. Andy loved working with pastels. Here is a list of his portfolios:

Charles Emil Ruckstuhl

PORTFOLIOS	YEAR	PUBLISHER
Colts and Champions	1955	Harper & Brothers
Look of a Thoroughbred	1963	Harper & Row
Grey, Bay and Chestnut	1952	Harper & Brothers
Before the Bugle	1968	Macmillan
Turf and Bluegrass	1950	Harper & Brothers
Bred to Run	1960	Harper & Brothers

Time's Distortion

St. Petersburg

As you look back in time, it appears, at least as I see it, that time between events seems stretched as if viewed through a telescope. For instance, from the time I met Andy to the time, say, when I got out of military school seems like decades rather than years. On the opposite end of the scale, what I call the accordion effect, the time between my return from South America until the sad day when he left the earth, seems very short. Therefore, this last short section of Andy's biography covers a rather long span of time.

Upon the retirement of my mother's physician, or general practitioner, Dr. Boynton (Bobcat's owner), mother acquired the services of another doctor, a young man, Dr. Larry

40

Churchville, who also lived and practiced in Townsend. That was a short time before I returned from my South American venture. Consequently, I acquired Churchville's services when it became advisable for me to have a checkup in view of the fact that I had had a bout with hepatitis that year. I had acquired a small apartment in Boston near Andy and my mother's winter residence at the time. During the vacation period I was taking after leaving Bendix International, I was trying out a new marketing venture with the Sylvania illuminating division.

Dr. Churchville checked me over and made two suggestions. The first involved a short stay at the Pratt Diagnostic Clinic where he suggested I have a liver biopsy to be sure all was in order. The second Churchville idea was the better, as I saw it.

"Chan," he said to me, waving his stethoscope, "I hate to see you bumming around Boston by yourself, living alone at Charlesgate West. You've been married once, and it's high time you thought about settling down to a normal life."

"What do you mean?" I asked.

"Well," he answered, looking upwards, as if philosophizing, "I think it's time you got together with someone I have known a long time, someone like you, a professional, charming person, a young lady from a fine family. She's a nurse. Her name is Muriel."

I said I would like to meet Muriel. Indeed I did! We went to a movie on a "blind date" and parted, rather miraculously, I thought, with a planned second date – New Year's Eve.

Andy always threw a New Year's eve party wherever he lived. This year, 1949, it would be in his Mason studio. It was the perfect place for me to fix up a grand audio system with a few dancing oscilloscopes to spread the musical charm around visually. With Andy's help, I rigged up some ultraviolet incandescent bulbs to add to the frivolity. They fluoresce objects such as shirt cloth – and so, the party was on.

Charles Emil Ruckstuhl

Andy met Muriel. The days began to light up. The months began to slip by quickly, and by July there was a wedding at a beautiful little granite church in Peterborough, N.H. A week later found the newlyweds in Germany, staying for a two-year honeymoon. But that wasn't the end of communication between the Andersons and us. Several evenings per week would find us at my amateur radio microphone, talking to Mason via a nearby amateur friend in Massachusetts. We never lost touch.

Madeleine and Andy began to travel. Their first travels were to St. Petersburg, Florida, to escape the worst of winter chills. I managed to establish a few business connections that took us to the warm state and afforded us time with the Andersons when the winds were blowing cold in New England. Time was flying fast. The highlights of the next few years included a hair-raising flight by the Andersons in a Constellation that nearly came apart in turbulent weather. The plane was grounded after landing.

Paris, April 21, 1956.

Later, my business allowed Muriel and me to have vacations in the Caribbean while the Andersons were in Florida. At about that time Muriel and I built a substantial home on a hill in Groton, Massachusetts, about 15 miles from Mason, so communication continued as usual. Then Madeleine and Andy began to travel to Europe where Andy could spend fruitful times at the Louvre and in Italy where art, according to Andy, may have been born.

While the Andersons were in France, on one of their several trips, I had made contact with a French radio amateur with whom we were able to arrange schedules to keep in contact. I had given my mother an Aiwa tape recorder that she deftly used to record her travels. On one trip with my radio friends, the Claveiroles, who lived on Rue de Vaugirard, my mother recorded my signals received by Andre Claveirole in his car while they were in Versailles.

Aboard the Leonardo da Vinci, 1966.

Although I couldn't hear his portable radio signals, mine were very strong and recorded on mother's Aiwa magnificently!

It is interesting that the Rue de Vaugirard was the street where my mother and I lived for a few weeks in Paris before getting a relatively permanent *"pied a terre"* in 1924.

The last years saw Andy's popularity continue, undiminished, but one day, in Mason, Andy noticed that Madeleine was becoming unduly forgetful. The end was coming. Mother was suffering from mitral stenosis that resulted in a series of small strokes that would eventually end her life.

Andy always arose before Madeleine. Separate bedrooms, which they always had, made arising at different times uncomplicated. As a daily ritual, Andy squeezed orange juice for Madeleine and put it on an upper shelf of the refrigerator. In a sort of celebration of this noble task, and the preparation of other nick-knacks on her breakfast tray, Andy always wrote a short humorous, whimsical poem for her to see when she was up and ready for her breakfast. He wrote 41 poems in 41 days. Mother was taken to the hospital, never to return after the 41ˢᵗ poem. These poems, taken from my book "The Last Breakfasts" are form a part of this biography.

Early one morning the telephone rang in Groton. It was Andy.

"Your mother passed away last night at Phillips House" (Massachusetts General Hospital). It was a terse announcement, and before I could say anything the line went dead. I could do nothing. Andy wanted nothing but he did continue, trying to finish what would be his last book, "The Conamara Pony".

One Morning, just 59 days later, Helene Guidone, a good friend whose apartment was on the floor below Andy's studio, heard a dull thud from above. Andy had been felled by a massive stroke and lay there, dead. The year: 1971.

A funeral took place that spring in Mason, N.H., where Andy and Madeleine lie beside each other in Mason's "new cemetery". The epitaph on Andy's gravestone reads:

"The world was richer for his coming, and poorer for his leaving."

Andy as I Knew Him

Andy's Last Picture, 1969

CHAPTER TWO

C. W. Anderson's
Humor of the Art Deco Era

Sketches and Doggerel Verse

Although C.W.Anderson was a well known artist of horses and author of books pertaining to horsemanship and horse lore, his subtle humor and his artistic talent in other directions were considerably less known.

During the 1920s and early 30s, Anderson lived in Greenwich Village, Manhattan, (at 41 Washington Square South). He graduated from the Chicago Art Institute after WW1 peace was declared and made a fair living drawing weekly cartoons for the New Yorker and Ballyhoo magazines. He also did some front covers for The Saturday Evening Post and for Youth's Companion. But horses had never crossed his path - not until 1926.

That was the year "Andy", as we called him, met my mother, Madeleine. She had been studying art in Paris for a year but had returned at Christmas time (1925) with me because of a detached retina that resulted from an accident in her art class. The two met at a Camp for "grown-ups" on Lake Kezar in Maine during the summer of 1926. It was here that their friendship was cemented for the next 44 years.

Madeleine's summer home in Mason, N.H., allowed her to keep a riding horse, Peter. Andy visited Mason, met Peter, and the rest is history. Although he continued to do cartoons, Andy slowly shifted his interest and talent toward horses.

Madeleine's divorce in 1931 allowed her to live close to Andy's studio on Washington Square. A mutual effort by both my mother and Andy resulted in numerous children's books that in time led to more serious books, paintings and pastels of racing champions. By 1936 Andy had completely shifted over to horses and children's books. His first book, titled "Billy and Blaze" was published in 1936 by Macmillan. Dozens of publications later, my mother also started writing children's books, illustrated by Andy. Macmillan liked them and published them too.

It is during the early days when Andy's transition occurred that we now place ourselves. Andy's sense of humor never ceased and thus, I have the rare pleasure to be able to put this booklet together for perhaps semisophisticated adult reading - "grown-up" is perhaps a better word.

Art deco was the rage. The Chrysler Building had just been completed and they were planning to tear down the Hotel Astor to make room for the Empire State Building. Sugar daddies were buying mink coats for their young mistresses and the milkman was making noises at 4 a.m. This is the platform on which the humor of these pages is based. This is a side of "Andy" few knew.

Andy

There was a little girl

And she had a little curl

Right in the middle of her forehead

When she was bad she was very, very nice

And when she was good she was horrid.

Charles Emil Ruckstuhl

There was an old lady who lived in a shoe,
She had so many children she didn't know what to do.
She read Margaret Sanger and now it's a scandal
She has plenty of room in an open toed sandal.

Lovely ankles, lovely thighs

And a glance from flashing eyes.

Invitation or derision?

Damn my astigmatic vision!

Charles Emil Ruckstuhl

Patty cake, Patty cake baker's man,
Run along as fast as you can,
Baby's dieting, Baby has hips,
If Baby sees pastry then Baby slips.

Literary Evening

First the Scotch and then the ice,
First the verse and then the vice,
And vice versa is also nice.

Charles Emil Ruckstuhl

Biological Urge

Roses are red,
Violets blue,
Temporarily,
I love you.

Mary had a little lamb.
"Mm-Mm - Mm!! said Mary.

Charles Emil Ruckstuhl

Some say naked,
Some say nude,
Some say naughty,
Some say lewd,
Depending on age
And rectitude.

Charles Emil Ruckstuhl

Rock a Bye Baby in the tree top.
No dishes to do, no cradle to rock,
When the stocks break the duplex will fall,
Down will come Baby, mink coat and all.

Andy as I Knew Him

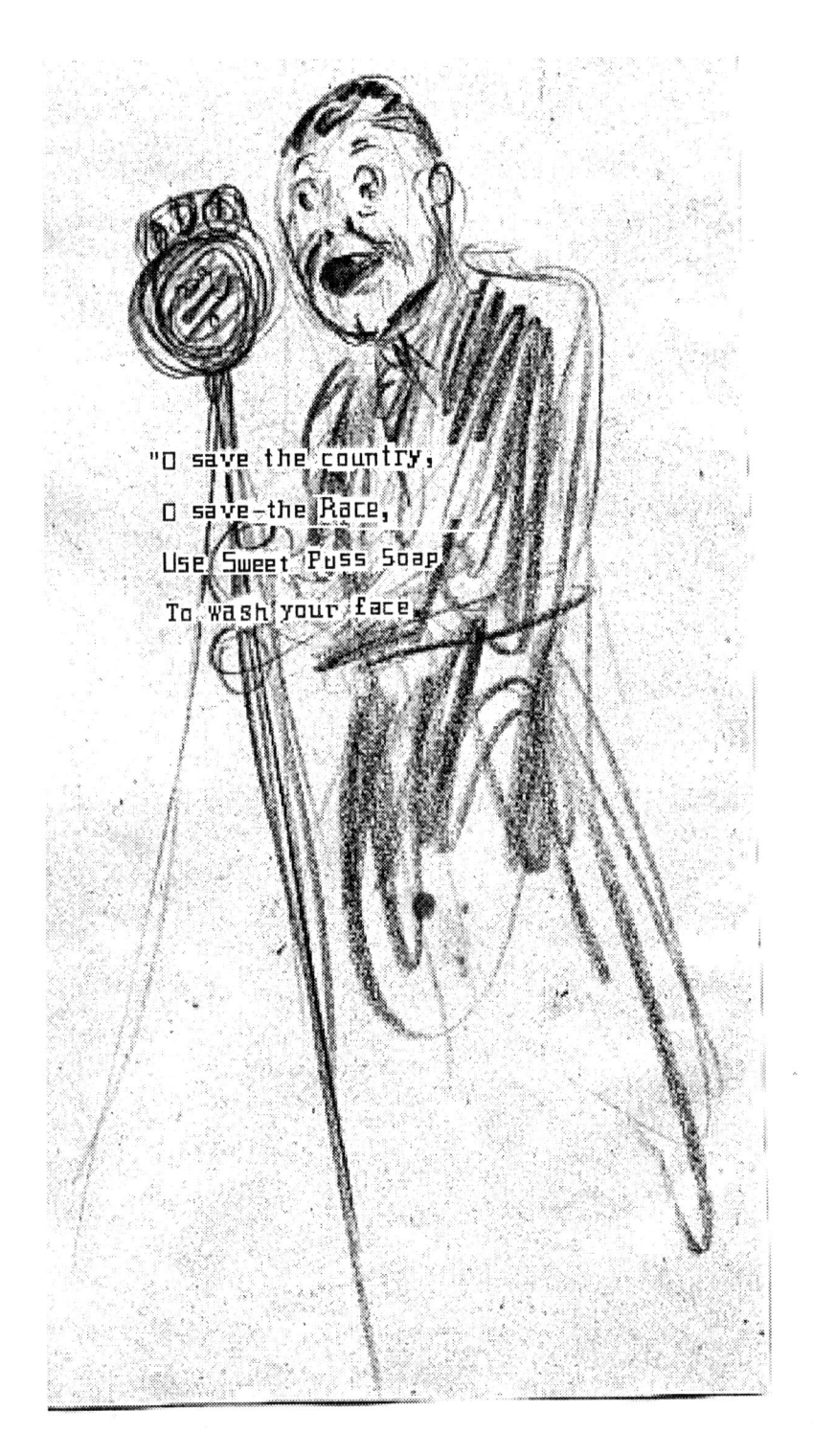

"O save the country,
O save the Race,
Use Sweet Puss Soap
To wash your face

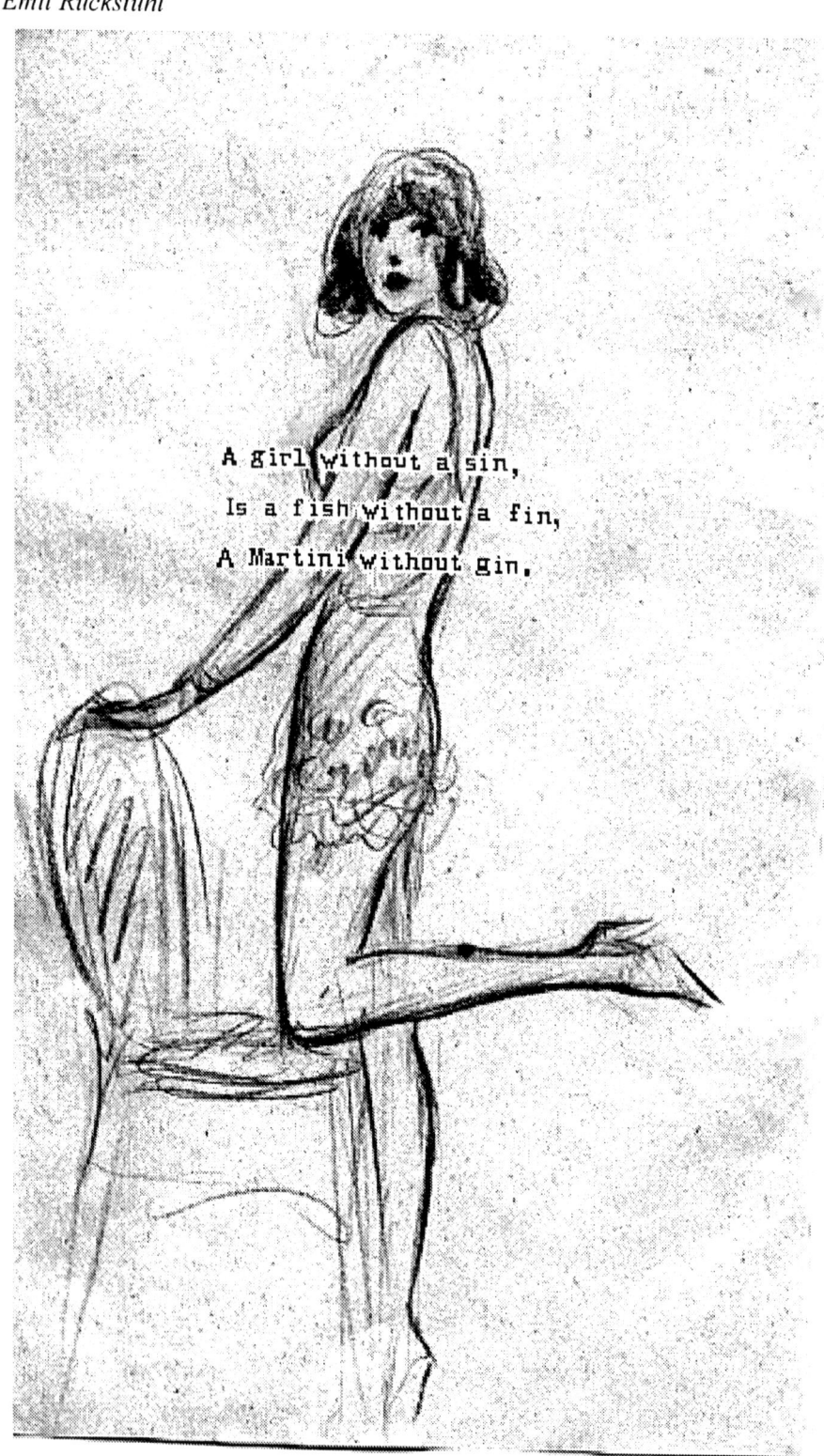

Charles Emil Ruckstuhl

A girl without a sin,
Is a fish without a fin,
A Martini without gin.

Andy as I Knew Him

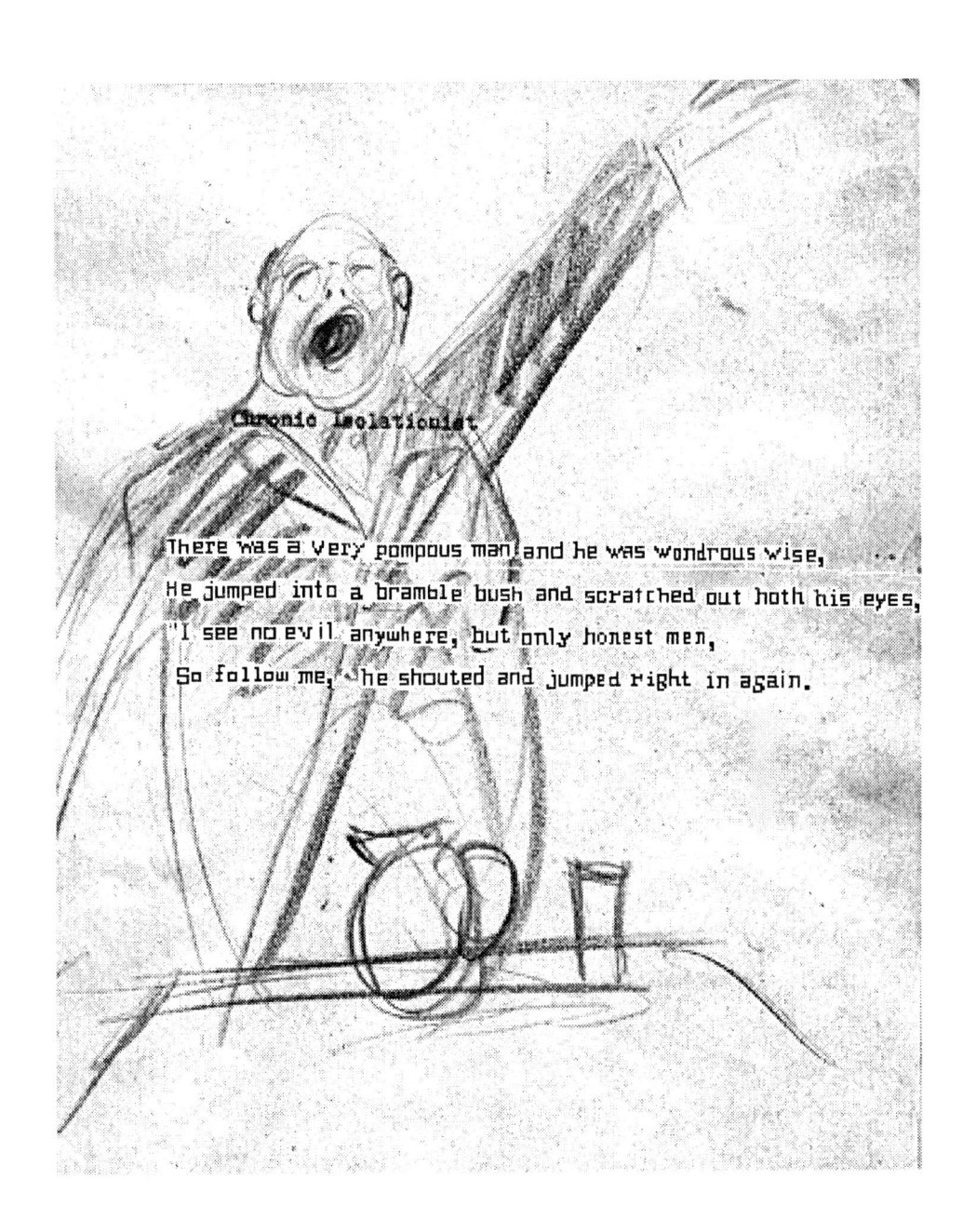

Chronic Isolationist

There was a very pompous man and he was wondrous wise,
He jumped into a bramble bush and scratched out both his eyes,
"I see no evil anywhere, but only honest men,
So follow me," he shouted and jumped right in again.

Charles Emil Ruckstuhl

Little Miss Muffet

Sat on a tuffet

Her escort was under the table.

Then came a fat spider

And sat down beside her

And now her tuffet is sable..

Andy as I Knew Him

Café Count

Ba Ba Black Sheep
Have you any wool
Yes Sir, yes Sir,
Three bags Full,

One is full of bad checks
One is full of duds,
A cardboard dickey
And phoney studs.

Charles Emil Ruckstuhl

> Sing a song of six pence,
> A pocket full of Rye.
> A dark brown taste
> And a bright red eye.

There was a crooked man
And he had a crooked spouse,
Lived on a crooked lane
And in a crooked house.

He straightened up the lane,
Rebuilt the crooked cottage.
Since what he sold his birthright for
Was no small mess of pottage.

Charles Emil Ruckstuhl

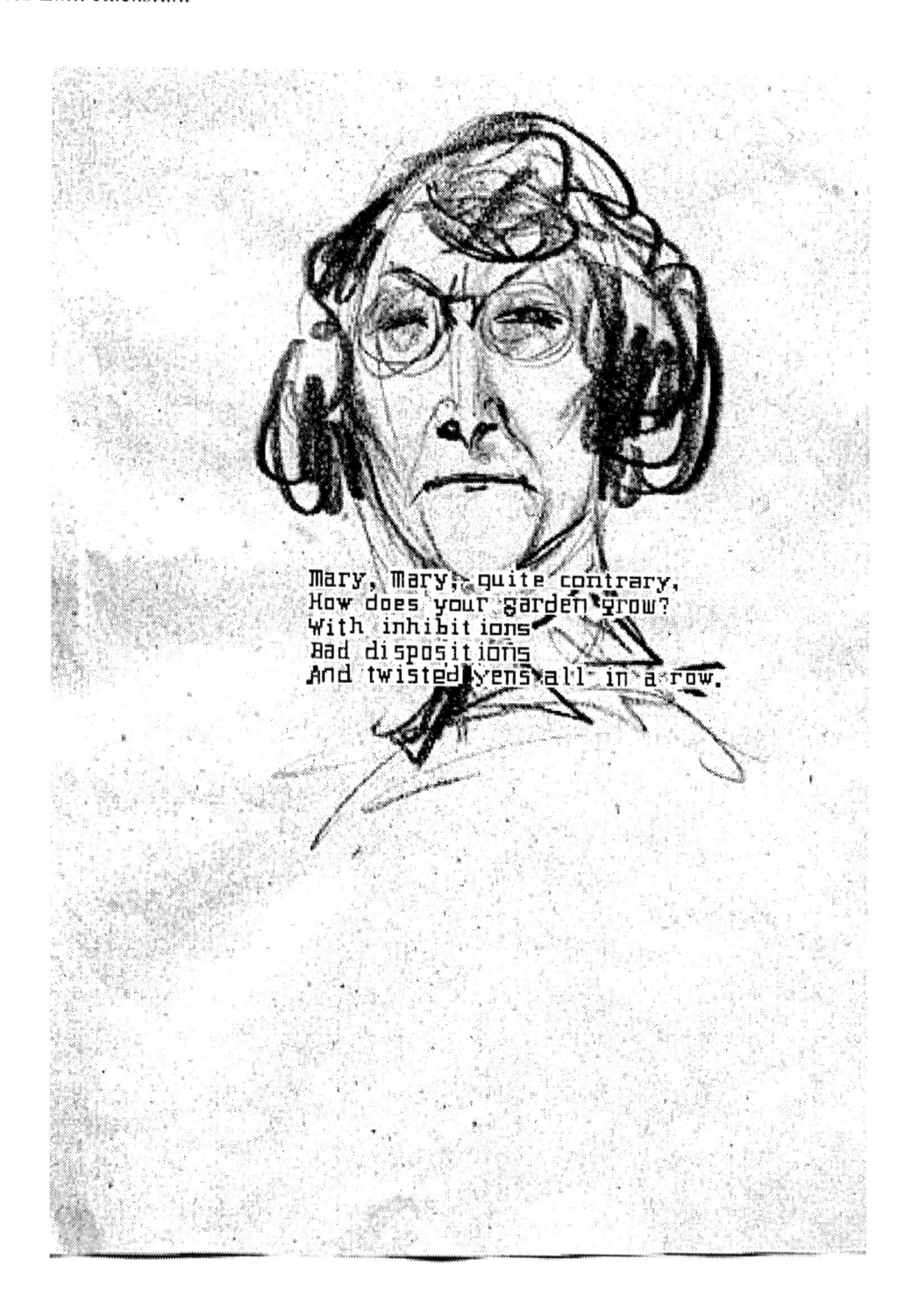

Mary, Mary, quite contrary,
How does your garden grow?
With inhibitions
Bad dispositions
And twisted yens all in a row.

> Bye Baby Bunting
> Daddy's gone a-hunting
> To find a little sable skin
> To wrap his baby Bunting in.

Charles Emil Ruckstuhl

Andy as I Knew Him

Charles Emil Ruckstuhl

Bread is the staff of life

(Sketches from Paris)

At the Louvre Museum of Art

Charles Emil Ruckstuhl

Modern Art The Mona Lisa

(At the Louvre)

Andy as I Knew Him

CHAPTER THREE
ANDY'S CARTOONING DAYS

Conde Nast Publications, with which The New Yorker is affiliated, has given me kind permission to use a number of Andy's cartoons, done for them in the 1926-1936 period. I have selected around three dozen of his sketches for inclusion here to show how Andy changed over the period. As you will see, he started with charcoal sketches, went to cartoons and, in the end, became a serious equine artist of great popularity and skill.

The dating of the pictures is as the New Yorker had them noted in their files.

The following cartoons were originally published in The New Yorker. For more information about The New Yorker please visit www.newyorker.com or www.cartoonbank.com.

Charles Emil Ruckstuhl

This is Andy's first submittal to the New Yorker magazine. It was submitted as a sort of decoration for their section on coming sports events. As in all of Andy's sketches, the grace and movement he portrays is strong evidence of his artistic capabilities.

Here we have the second non-cartoon submission to The New Yorker by C.W. Anderson. It was not submitted as a cartoon as such, but rather as a sort of decoration for the New Yorker's summary of musical events, dances, balls, and the like. (The New Yorker's internal notation, the date, has been purposely retained just as they filed it.)

Andy's training in Chicago and his own talent are shown in the graceful rendition of two people dancing in perfect unison and symmetry.

Andy as I Knew Him

This is Andy's first submittal of a cartoon to The New Yorker. It followed the skater drawing by only a few weeks and made a hit with the publishers. The Volstead act was still in effect, and would be for another six years. Prohibition had become somewhat of a joke. This fact made it all the more amusing to see two gals looking in a department store window that featured a cocktail shaker and four cocktail glasses. The contents were prohibited but not the containers! Orangeade anyone?

This was the year Andy became interested in horses, thanks to his having met Madeleine that summer up on Lake Kezar. This is one of three horse-oriented sketches he submitted to the New Yorker, two serious in nature, and this one, humorous as the gentleman with the crop is ogling other than the subjects on display.

Charles Emil Ruckstuhl

These two sketches, submitted at the same time as the "ogler", show that, he had, at this early stage of his interest in horses, an exact and correct feel for the animal's structure and composition. The subjects are not rounded as in the finished product, but the basics are there. Little did we know what lay ahead for Mr. C.W. Anderson as he applied himself to this facet of the world of art.

"Yes - - - you know it would be cheap if it weren't so frightfully expensive."

Here we go with the first of Andy's cartoons that portrays a particular kind of sense of humor. Andy found his humor in everyday conversation and this cartoon is no exception. If he heard something that had the slightest ring of humor to it, Andy would pounce upon it, repeat it, embellish it and finish it off with his contagious way of laughing. You never could tell if it might be in the next month's New Yorker.

Ballyhoo was the second magazine for which Andy supplied his priceless humor, but, unfortunately, nothing remains of what became Dell Publishing Company's humorous magazine in its last days. It's all gone. How I wish I had the funniest of all cartoons (I think) that he drew. It was of an Indian with a blanket, sending up a smoke signal, turning to his partner with a quizzical look on his face, asking "How do you spell Ugh?"

Charles Emil Ruckstuhl

Here we go, a little more than a year after Andy submitted his first drawings to The New Yorker. This cartoon explains in part what Andy had to say about the new art-humor form It was that the sketch must contain its own humor, or most of it - a constraint, as opposed to the old-fashioned delivery of words that simply had a picture accompanying them. (Again, we leave the New Yorker's notations and filing data intact).

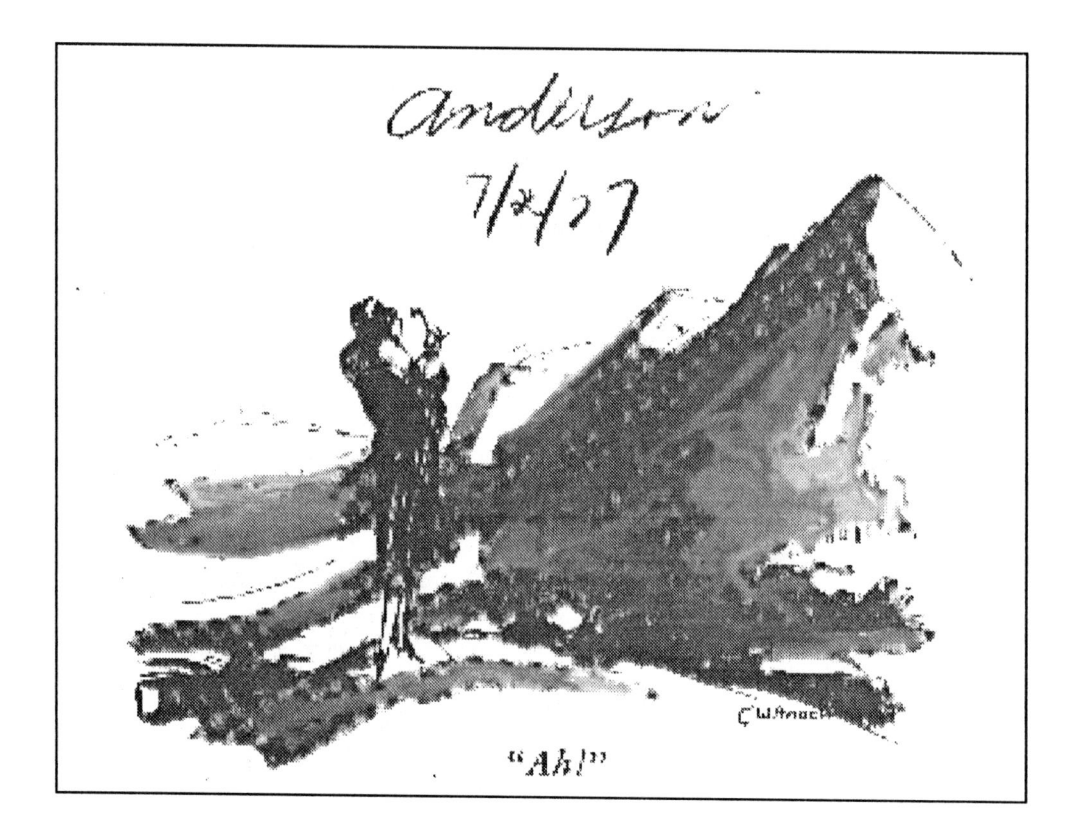

"Ah!"

> "Here's one for a poil diver."
> "Probably filled by now—it's nine o'clock."

Andy is producing abundant cartoons for both the New Yorker and Ballyhoo. These two drawings are typical of the sense of humor of the day and perhaps not too far removed from today's humor.

Andy made a lot of his drawings in the park at Washington Square and it shows in this and the following drawing.

Charles Emil Ruckstuhl

"Nice day, ain't it, Joe?"

MAY 21 1927

You can't go much beyond this for simplicity of humor. Man-hole covers and day laborers haven't changed in three-quarters of a century. People still smoke pipes and sit on their shovels. Skirt lengths seem to be about the same and little trees still grow in metropolitan areas. The New Yorker hasn't changed all that much – it is only we, young at the time of this publication, that have changed!

Andy as I Knew Him

No one today would be able to understand this cartoon without knowledge of crime history. On March 27, 1927, Ruth Snyder murdered her husband with a window sash weight. We don't have sash weights any more but back in 1927 they were used to counterweight one's windows for easy opening and shutting. A sash weight is about two feet long and about an inch and a half in diameter. It is made of cast iron and, if properly handled, makes a terrific night-stick! After a very long trial and investigations out to kazoo, Ruth was found guilty of murdering her husband and was electrocuted in Sing-Sing on January 22, 1928. The story kept the Daily News and the New York Mirror in business for many months. I recall the murder case well, as did many of my schoolmates who felt they were witnesses to a real murder story instead of something fabricated for a paperback book.

The three sketches below are Anderson rarities. Andy didn't do dogs often. The only other rendition of dogs, done by Andy, exists as a painting of a hound in a collection unknown to me. He also did a pastel of a hound that is part of a portfolio published by Harper Brothers. He did paint other dogs, but only as a part of a hunting sports event: The Groton Hunt. Andy's one, and most singular cat, appears on the next page.

Charles Emil Ruckstuhl

I should not overlook Andy's poodle that expresses his judgement of the creature, adorned by human beings. I thought this was a raging bull, but it turned out to be just a French poodle.

And finally, the cat – oblivious to the rest of the world and happy wherever it finds food, companionship and love.

Now we are getting into the era when everything was accelerating toward that outrageous day, some 16 months ahead, when the stock market would take its dive and people would start jumping out of windows in total despair, after losing their paper fortunes. Humor, however, was a commodity with an iron shell, impervious to market conditions. And so it was with this and other drawings submitted by Andy. Each fetched around $100 when $100 went a very long way. Oranges were 27 cents a dozen and butter was the same per pound. Taxi charges were 15 cents for the first quarter mile and 5 cents for each succeeding quarter-mile. A 10 cent tip was OK.

He never knew why she said "No."

Here, once again, we have the dry humor of the day. Antiques were a popular collector's sport and most anything that resembled an antique might be said to have great value even if the beauty and utility were totally absent. One might question "Where is the rest of the bed?" But patience, to prevent the murmur soon replies . . . . .

Charles Emil Ruckstuhl

"Now this is a very lovely bed."

7-21-26

This is a perfect example of our Anderson quotation earlier in this book (Chapter 1). A cartoon should contain all the information possible in the drawing itself. This one surely does, as our poor messenger "boy" rides the subway to his delivery destination.

Andy as I Knew Him

"Rhinelander
0-five-nine-six."

Charles Emil Ruckstuhl

"*I'm afraid Huntley is finding the symbolism a little obscure.*"

The humor in this cartoon isn't so much in what is being said or how it is being said. It lies in the expression of dear old "Huntley", a victim of two circumstances: one, the show itself, which must have been deadly, and, two, the entourage on either seat beside him. One can almost feel the inner urgency of Huntley's desire to be anywhere but in this predicament.. Here again, the better part of the humor is in the drawing, not the text.

Andy as I Knew Him

"I don't remember the name – it's about a girl who wants to live her own life."

> You don't have to turn many pages to reach the dry humor represented in this cartoon by Andy. One can just imagine what the bookstore manager is thinking when confronted by this request. It is safe to say that what he is thinking cannot be written on any keyboard. There are no letters for the keys represented here!

Charles Emil Ruckstuhl

"Do you think a pair of gloves would be too much?"

Retailers must have loved this one! With excessive ornamentations that have nothing to do with the subject, the designer asks if a pair of gloves would be too much!

The humor of self-deprecation was highly accepted in these days of "anything goes".

Andy as I Knew Him

"It just hasn't got it."

Andy drew a lot of his sketches in the Washington park from which you could see this building, the Brevoort Hotel, down on the East side of lower Fifth Avenue. Self-deprecation again sneaks into the humor!

Charles Emil Ruckstuhl

"What's his name?"
"I don't know. Just met him lately."

Dry humor, wet humor – you name it. This cartoon defines the flapper philosophy of the roaring twenties. Take it or leave it!

Andy as I Knew Him

"*I wouldn't have taken him back, would you?*"

There is nothing much that you can add to make this anything but hilarious. The woman on the left has obviously made the old maidish remark, befitting her appearance!

Charles Emil Ruckstuhl

Give the telephone credit for making this cartoon as amusing as it is. One might suggest that the caller, undoubtedly a handsome male, stick to his guns in the pursuit of his "horrid" goals!

Andy as I Knew Him

"*It was right on this spot, Albert, where you first tried to kiss me and I was so offended.*" AUG 2 1930

With a couple of kids wrapped around his neck, Albert, who is trying to read the newspaper, may wish he never tried to steal that first kiss from the lady of his dreams who, trying to be pleasantly reminiscing, is making the scene just that more difficult to bear!

Charles Emil Ruckstuhl

> We have something fairly straightforward here, for a change!

Andy as I Knew Him

"Shall I smile?"

JUL 2 1932

Once again we are obeying the Anderson rule of having most of the humor right in the cartoon itself!

Charles Emil Ruckstuhl

"I can't understand why you don't like these hills, Wilmer."

Andy as I Knew Him

JUL 1 1933

"Do you mind if I call you pardner?"

This page does not need to be clarified!.

Charles Emil Ruckstuhl

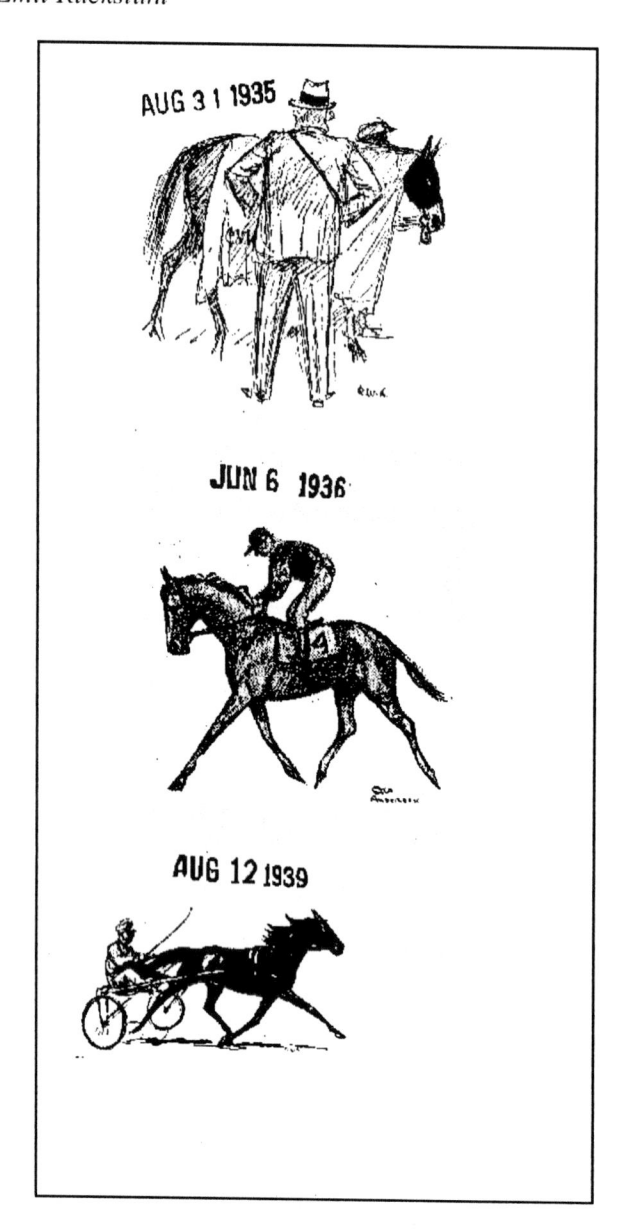

This last set of sketches, when compared with the first renditions of the same subject years earlier, show how Andy improved his portrayal of the equine world. Andy became so successful by the mid-thirties that he no longer had time to stay in the world of cartoons. One loss was by far offset by a subsequent gain for the world.

CHAPTER FOUR
THE LAST BREAKFASTS.

Drawings and Poems Written by C. W. Anderson to His Dying Wife

Charles Emil Ruckstuhl

ANDY
THE LAST BREAKFASTS.

C.W. Anderson, famous horse author and artist, wrote these 41 poetic notes at his breakfast table in Mason, N.H. Once a day, he left one on the tray he had prepared for his late rising wife, Madeleine, my mother. September and October 1970 had arrived and mother was failing rapidly. She passed away just after the last poem, number 41.

These whimsical poems by Anderson, based on his freshly squeezed "orange juice" theme, portray his love for my mother, his sadness and his sensitivity, as well as his ever-present sense of humor. Mother and "Andy" loved this time of year when they took their daily horseback rides through the flaming countryside colors, savoring their union and their presence on earth to its fullest.

These poems represent a sort of farewell, an outpouring of tenderness and humor blended in an accolade to their life together. They speak clearly of his devotion to the lady who helped make C.W.Anderson the great author and artist he was. It was she who sparked his genius 45 years earlier, when they first met.

These poems also portray a side of "Andy" that was known only to his family and close friends. His poems and his sketches (one included for each poem) were done from 1927 to the 1960s. A humorous side of "Andy" is also portrayed in the chapter devoted to Anderson's humorous sketches. These are accompanied by short verses befitting the 1930's when sugar daddies were immortalized in song, on the stage and in cartoons.

Anderson was born in Wahoo, Nebraska in 1892. He died in Boston in 1970, perhaps of a broken heart, a mere few months after Madeleine passed away.

"Andy", as my family called him, ("Herc" by his family because of his height of 6' 4") specialized in thoroughbred horses. His books and his portfolios of pastels were published by Macmillan and by Harper Brothers respectively. He also wrote books that addressed themselves to horsemanship and its instructional aspects, all illustrated by the genius of his hand. Many other popular children's books, published by Macmillan, were written by my mother, Madeleine, and illustrated by Andy.

Notes: (1) "Ruth" in these poems was Ruth Newell, housemaid, who lived in Mason. (2) Anderson pen and ink drawings of trees, 1968. Others, 1927.

Charles Emil Ruckstuhl

Madeleine and Andy

Berkshire Foothills

Charles Emil Ruckstuhl

September 7, 1970.

The orange juice is in the refrigerator.

The sun is again in the sky.

And I still love you.

Nearby Maple Tree

Charles Emil Ruckstuhl

September 8.

The orange juice is in the usual place,

And so is the sun.

My heart is still on my sleeve,

Which is rather worn and the nap is gone.

But not from my heart.

Maple Tree

Charles Emil Ruckstuhl

September 9.

No sun today.

No Ruth.

Only orange juice in ice box. And love in my heart

Port on Long Island

Charles Emil Ruckstuhl

September 10

The sun is hid and the sky forlorn,

And Ruth now labors in alien corn,

Although I offend both scent and sight

My little candle I keep alight.

And the orange juice is at hand.

Very Old Maple Tree

Charles Emil Ruckstuhl

<u>*No Date (but all in sequence)*</u>

The rain comes down from leaden skies,

Nature's gift in drab disguise.

And Mason's gift -

Our Ruth is here.

So what is left

To wish for dear?

And the orange juice

Is in the ice box.

Old Maple Tree

September 16.

The rain is done
And it may turn fine
And Ruth is here at
Half past nine.
And I must go to
The vintner's lair
For two dozen flagons
Of rosé rare.
And the juice of the
Orange is again in there.

Long Island Sound 1927

September 19.

The sun shines bright

In our old New Hampshire home.

It's autumn and the

Foliage is gay.

The oranges are ripe and

The juice is on the shelf.

And Ruth scours your

Troubles all away.

Young Beech

September 20.

The sun's in the sky.
The juice on the shelf
And I'm in the kitchen
All by myself.
And Ruth is at play
Or what passes for play
In the Newell abode
On a full holiday.

Old Maple

Charles Emil Ruckstuhl

<u>*No Date (but next in series)*</u>

The sun shines bright,

A new day is born

An d Ruth is still

Amidst alien corn.

When hunger gnaws

She will be here,

And you are still

My dearest dear.

And the orange juice

Is in the ice box.

Central Park

September 23.

The wind makes the trees
A billowing sea;
An inland ocean
For you and me.
The day is balmy,
Fair and clear.
A day for your shooting stick
My dear.

The Old Bucaneer Yellow Maple)

Charles Emil Ruckstuhl

September 26.

The morning sky

Is overcast.

The sun may come

Or the clouds may last.

But whether the sky

Is gray or blue

My old heart warms

Itself near you.

Healthy Maple

September 27.

It showered last night
But I don't know when
And the morning brings
Back summer again.
The juice is as always
On its usual shelf
And I am always
My constant self.

CWA's Only Cat Drawing

Charles Emil Ruckstuhl

<u>No Date.</u>

The day breaks dull and

Gray forsooth

And I must be

Your erstwhile Ruth.

So I carefully scrub each

Pan and pot

Partly a maid and partly

Not.

Another Maple

Charles Emil Ruckstuhl

September 28.

The morning's chill
And the air is clear
With glimpses of sun
For you, my dear.
To bring to the leaves
A more glowing gold
To take the edge
From the morning cold.
And the juice is really in
The ice box.

Midlife Maple

September 29.

Autumn is back in view again.

She was pushed off stage

By summer's last fling.

The leaves grow brighter

And the air is crisp.

And my heart is warm

Although no birds sing.

And the orange juice is in

The ice box.

Madeleine 1927

Charles Emil Ruckstuhl

September 30.

The morning has October chill

Although September lingers still.

The crimson and gold that greets our eyes

Is a last farewell as the summer dies.

And the orange juice again

Awaits you.

Yellow Maple

Charles Emil Ruckstuhl

October 3.

Grayer and grayer the leaden skies;

A different gray than your gray eyes.

The gray sky promises cold and rain,

But your gray eyes are the sun again.

And the juice of the orange awaits you.

Yet Another Maple

Charles Emil Ruckstuhl

October 4.

This autumn day is cool and clear.

A day for you, my dearest dear.

A stain of color spreads over the hill

And my heart hears a song

Though the birds are still.

Long Island Sound 1927

October 5.

Without my rose colored glasses on

The sky is gray and the sun is wan

But flowers in the garden

Still make a brave show.

Do you think they know

Of frost and snow?

Solitary Maple

Charles Emil Ruckstuhl

First Friday in October.

The mist hangs low

And damp and cold.

A day when body and heart

Feel old.

It grays down even

The brightest hue.

But it cannot gray

My thoughts of you.

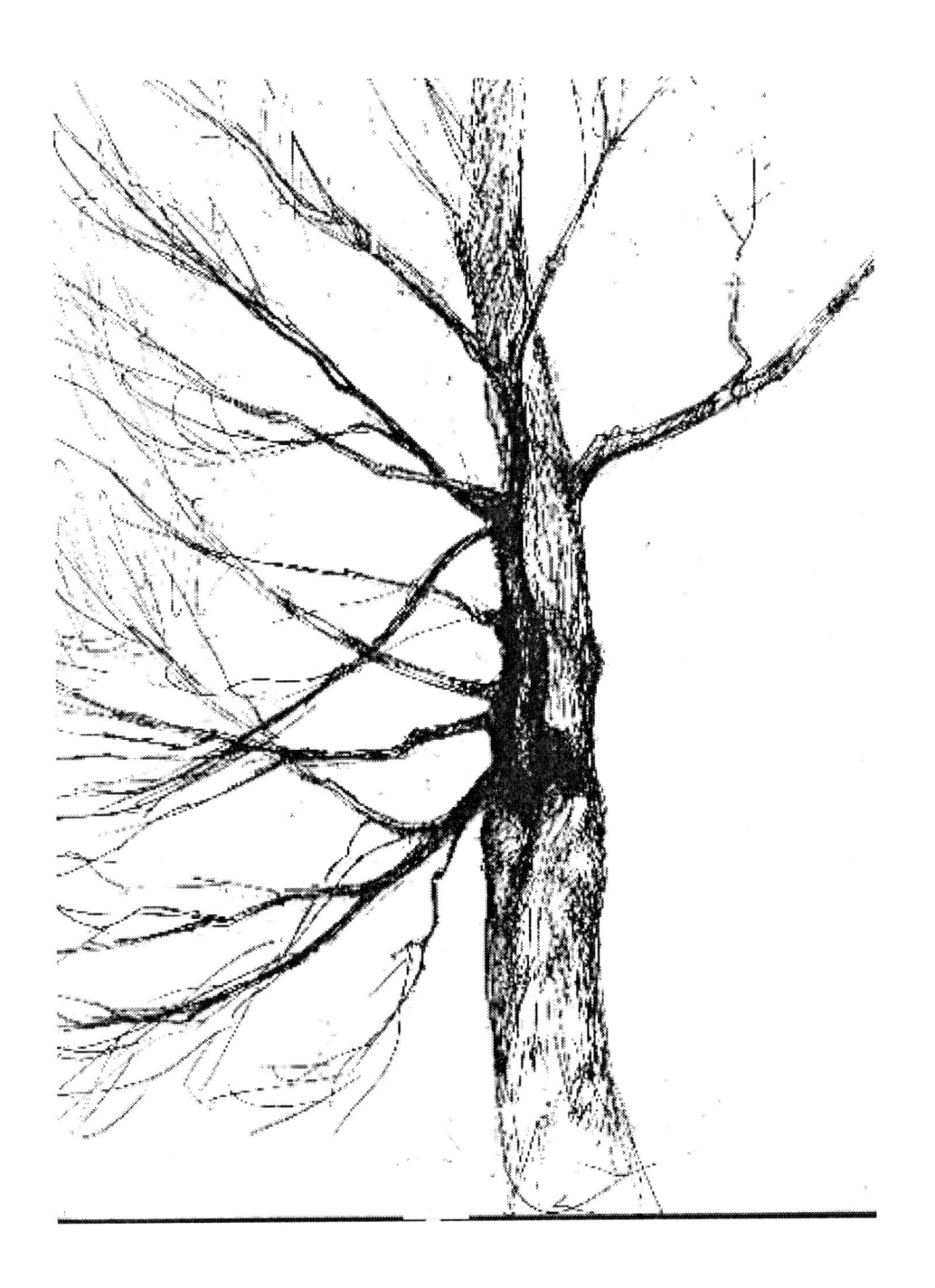

Windblown Maple

Charles Emil Ruckstuhl

October 7.

Nature's quieter pallet

Can now be seen.

Burnished bronze

And olive green.

But I saw a dash

Of scarlet now,

Like a tropical bird

On an autumn bough

And the juice of the orange awaits you.

Long Island Rocky Shore

No Date.

I have labored long

And I hope not in vain.

To do a child's small book again.

And now I send it

Upon its way.

So this, my dear,

Is a red letter day

And the juice.......

Sturdy Maple

Charles Emil Ruckstuhl

Still No Date.

The day is bright and clear and cold.

And more of the green has turned to gold.

Here and there a maple flames.

There are other colors that have no names.

Sturdy Giant

Charles Emil Ruckstuhl

October 9.

Today I feel as gay as a bird.

An elderly bird with arthritic wing.

My plumage is dull and my movements slow

And only my heart knows how to sing.

But the juice is fresh……..

Old Dock, Long Island

Charles Emil Ruckstuhl

October 10.

The world today is gray on gray.

No trace of color comes through the mist.

And so it is not a cheerful day.

A feeling of gloom is hard to resist.

But still the sun is somewhere there,

A mile or two in clearer air.

Hillside Maple

October 11.

Again the day is dark and damp.

The world but an unlighted lamp.

But through the years I have come know

You must depend on an inner glow.

(Har-har writes Madeleine)

And the orange juice is bright on the shelf.

Perfect Maple

Charles Emil Ruckstuhl

October 12.

This gray on gray on gray on gray

Is not night so it must be day.

No grandiose thoughts from an inner fire

Can bring a tune from my dampened lyre.

But the juice is bright and sweet.

More Long Island, 1927

October 13.

Again gray skies

And a day forlorn.

And Ruth is in semi-

Alien corn.

But the orange is sweet

And its juice is here.

And so are you,

My dearest dear.

Established Maple

Charles Emil Ruckstuhl

October 14.

Nature's pallet is bright today

With all the colors that glow and burn,

And touches of brown and smoldering reds

And colors that painters never learn,

With here and there a rich dark green -

A laggard tree that forgets to turn.

But the juice of orange is golden.

Ancient Giant

Charles Emil Ruckstuhl

October 14 (Written by Madeleine on the back of the previous poem)

Woodbine is bright over the wall.
Bluejays give forth their raucus call.
Faint tones of autumn light far on the hill,
Low in the valley swamp willows flame still.

(Her last poem)

Somewhere in the Berkshires

Charles Emil Ruckstuhl

October Lament. (15th.)

The rain comes down from leaden skies.

A gray mist covers the red and gold.

Perchance the sun will shine again

But today I and the world are old.

"But today the world and I are old" corrects Madeleine

The Giant Falls asleep

Charles Emil Ruckstuhl

October 16.

I cannot find a rhyme today

Under these skies of sodden gray.

The sun will shine but who knows when?

I think I'll go back to bed again.

Young Ash

Charles Emil Ruckstuhl

<u>No Date.</u>

The day is clear
And the breeze is high.
With scarcely a cloud
In the pale blue sky.
But whether the sky
Be gray or blue
My thoughts are never
Far from you.

Willow

No Date.

October comes in under leaden skies.

The world is cold and no birds sing.

But the gold in the hill reminds me of you.

And my heart is a bell about to ring.

I cannot offer you power and pelf.

Only the juice on the topmost shelf.

Ash

October 17.

The sun shines brightly
And of rain no trace
While Ruth scrubs and
Shines in another place.
The orange is firm
And its juice is bright
And I dream of you
By day and night.

Sugar Maple

October 18.

The sky is gray and

Drips at seven.

And our Ruth comes

At half past eleven.

The orange juice on the

Topmost shelf

Is my only gift

Except myself.

Late Fall

Charles Emil Ruckstuhl

October 19.

The wind is sharp

But air is clear

And gone are the frogs

Of yesteryear.

The smoldering hill

Has burst into flame

And my spirit and heart

Are warm again.

("Andy", at end, scribbled by Madeleine. Her last written word.)

Beech

October 20.

Simple Palette

The road's aglow with gold and green,
As lovely a sight as I have seen.
How it was done I'll never know,
Just gold and green and such a glow.

The Young Ones

Charles Emil Ruckstuhl

Late October.

The road now has a deeper glow,
An older gold more thinly spread,
Deeper the carpet under foot
And bluer the skies are overhead.
A faint design becomes more bold,
Intricate patterns etched on gold.

Full Maple

Charles Emil Ruckstuhl

October 30.

The tapestry is faded now.

Just here and there a bright thread shows.

The bones of the trees show clearer now

As winter comes and autumn goes.

The distant hill no longer flames,

Just ashes and embers before the snows.

Winter's Sleep

Charles Emil Ruckstuhl

October 31.

The sky is blue

And the air is cold.

The day is new

But the year is old

And copper shows through

Yesteryear's gold.

MADELEINE

Charles Emil Ruckstuhl

No Date.

The sun shines bright.

But not for me.

Nature is but gray on gray.

Gold and red I do not see

For my honey is away.

Andy as I Knew Him

Author's note:

The last words written by Madeleine to her son were among the poems in this book. They read (referring to my piano):

"Leaves come tumbling down 'round my head'"... Remember? And "Scarecrow"? Do keep on playing. Love, Mother.

Madeleine's final poem was also among the last of Andy's breakfast poems. She must have known she was departing – that she was going home.

"Now, turning time, take what you must-
Quickness to move, to hear, to see.
When dust is drawing near to dust,
Such diminution need must be.
Yet leave, Oleane exempt from plunder,
My curiosity, my wonder."

Home

The humorous sketches and doggerel verses I recall were given to Madeleine in the early 1930s when she was ill. These have been assembled for posterity in Chapter Two, "C.W.Anderson's Art Deco Days Humor". My mother considered some of this material humorous. Some, not. Thus did "Andy's" product of diversion and musings rest for three-quarters of a century

CHAPTER FIVE
APPLICABLE MISCELLANY.

The following illustrations will add to the details in this book regarding Andy's progress from his early stages of endeavor to his state of perfection toward the last half of his life. One of Andy's art styles in the 1920s was a steel needle on a copper plate. He did not make many etchings, consequently these modes of presentation are rare today. Here is one etching Andy drew of my mother in Mason in 1927, playing our square piano. It should be noted that you cannot make a mistake when making an etching. Copper doesn't erase. Lithography, Andy's perhaps most abundant form of art does not permit errors either. Black wax on prepared stone cannot be erased.

Charles Emil Ruckstuhl

Etching of Madeleine in Mason, N.H., in 1927

Andy as I Knew Him

This is the real square piano in the Mason, N.H. house. Like most square pianos, it had a wooden frame that, by the physical standards of a piano that is supposed to keep its tuning, was pure rubber. A change in temperature or, especially, humidity would make for uncomfortable playing. I know. I played this piano often when I was a child in the learning stage,

The Blacksmith shop in Greenville, N.H. Gone since 1935

Much of Andu's work was associated with Mason and its vicinity. His trees, pines and deciduous varieties were all in Mason. Andy especially liked the blacksmith shop in next-door Greenville. It was there that his first horseshoes were forged and tailored to Madeleine's and his horses. But the day of the horse for commercial work was coming to and end and things were getting slow for the poor old blacksmith in Greenville. At first, Andy thought the idle blacksmith in his chair would provide the message but I suggested that a passing automobile would leave no doubt as to Andy's message. Andy liked the idea as you can see.

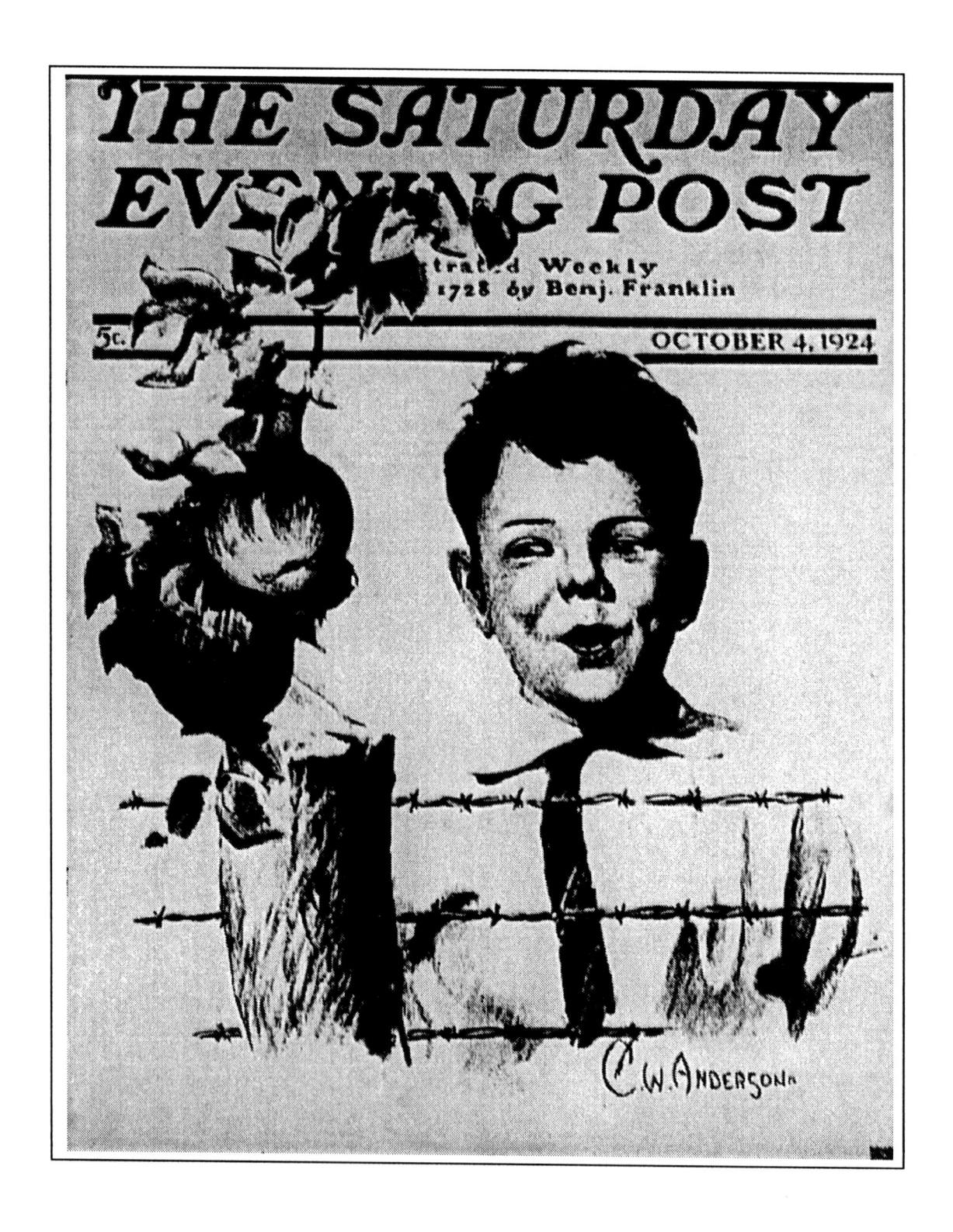

Charles Emil Ruckstuhl

Andy as I Knew Him

Andy's talent didn't go unappreciated as early as 1924 when he drew this picture of a young boy salivating at the thought of biting into a delicious apple on the wrong side of the barbed fence. Back in those days Andy signed his work in capital letters, distinctly different from later on.

Charles Emil Ruckstuhl

    This American beauty is one of four copies of Andy's work for the 1923 American Magazine. Smiling seductively over an empty champagne glass, this girl must have sold many copies of the issue.

ABOUT THE AUTHOR

Charles Ruckstuhl is an M.I.T. graduate engineer with a Phillips Exeter Academy graduate background. This combination has led him to publication in The Washington Times magazine World and I. He has also been published in The Groton Landmark newspaper with a monthly historical column on Groton. He has also written in The Monadnock Ledger, The Exeter Review, Reminisce, and in the New York Times. Ruckstuhl has published the book Forgotten Tales of Groton, an earlier version of Andy as I Knew Him and has started a magazine Spare Moments. Ruckstuhl is trilingual. At one time he spoke only French. He plays the piano, guitar and bass and has written some 50 popular jazz pieces. He is also an amateur radio operator and astronomer.